Great Tales and
Curiosities from
"The Silver State"

D1518954

Library of Congress Control Number: 2023938765

ISBN: 9781681064765

All photos are courtesy of the author or in the public domain unless otherwise noted.

Printed in the United States of America
23 24 25 26 27   5 4 3 2 1

Great Tales and
Curiosities from
"The Silver State"

AMAZING
NEVADA

SEVEN MAGIC MOUNTAINS, THE BEST IN THE WEST RIB
COOK-OFF, AND THE MAN WHO KILLED HIS KILLER

JANICE OBERDING

REEDY PRESS

Contents

CHAPTER 4

That's Quirky, Nevada 57

CHAPTER 5
Nevada Things to See and Do 113

Acknowledgments

Special thanks to my husband Bill whose help with this book was invaluable, and to Reedy Press' Jill Eccher and Barbara Northcott who have worked tirelessly, prodding and pushing me to make this book a wonderful reality.

Introduction

The 36th state added to the United States, Nevada is unique and varied. From the bright lights of the world-famous entertainment capital, Las Vegas, to the tiny town of Eureka, Nevada is rich in a history that includes miners, cowboys, gangsters, and women's rights activists. With its Native American heritage, Nevada is a state of legends and lore, a state with a fascinating history and a plethora of things to see and do. As you will soon read in the following pages, Nevada truly is an amazing state. But don't take my word for it; let me show you just how amazing the Silver State truly is.

Patricia "Pat" Nixon

Chapter One

Nevada's Amazing People

A state is nothing without its people. So it is with Nevada. Those included here were trailblazers, politicians, and pioneers. Some were ordinary people caught up in extraordinary events. Not all were upstanding and law abiding, but each and every one of them helped to shape Nevada into the culturally rich and unique place it is today. This is by no means a complete list of all Nevada's amazing people. For that, we would need several volumes.

The Ancestral Puebloans

Let's start at the beginning with the first people to live in this place we call Nevada—the Ancestral Puebloans. Thousands of years before Europeans came in their quest for fur and later gold and silver, the Ancestral Puebloans lived in what is today Southern Nevada. That's right! Millions of people visit Las Vegas every year. And while they ogle the many sights and sounds that are Las Vegas, they probably don't have a clue that about 50 miles (give or take) away is Overton and the Lost City Museum.

The Lost City Museum in Overton is located on a site where the ancient Ancestral Puebloans lived. The museum was built in 1935 by the Civilian Conservation Corps as a place to maintain and display Ancestral Puebloan artifacts that were discovered at the nearby Pueblo Grande de Nevada (Lost City) archaeological site. With the creation of Hoover Dam and man-made Lake Mead, most of the Lost City would eventually be beneath water.

Courtesy of tadam via Wikimedia Commons

The historical significance of the Ancestral Puebloans could not be ignored; crews worked frantically to save as many of the artifacts as possible.

The Ancestral Puebloans were peaceful people who lived along the Muddy and Virgin Rivers near present-day Overton. They made utilitarian use of baskets they wove from yucca plants and willows. They hunted deer, bighorn sheep, lizards, and rabbits using a primitive weapon known as an atlatl or spear thrower. Over time they would develop a more effective way of hunting game, the bow and arrow, and their utensils would be made of the more practical clay. An industrious people, they raised crops such as corn, cotton, and beans and mined turquoise and salt as valuable commodities. And then, as quickly as they had come, the Ancestral Puebloans left the region. Archaeologists still don't know why they left the area so abruptly or where they went.

Discovery of a Lifetime

In 1924, while prospecting for gold in a remote area of the Southern Nevada desert near the tiny town of Overton, two brothers, Fay and John Perkins, stumbled upon the remnants of a lost civilization. Excited by their find, the Perkinses rushed home to notify Nevada Governor James Scrugham. Luckily for all involved, Scrugham was a former state engineer and realized the importance of the brothers' discovery. The job of excavating this large site that would become known as Pueblo Grande de Nevada or the Lost City was not a job for amateurs. Scrugham contacted noted archaeologist M. R. Harrington of the Heye Foundation (the Museum of the American Indian) in New York for help in the excavation and study of the area. Southern Nevada became the focus of worldwide attention as the discovery of the Pueblo Grande de Nevada came to light.

Sarah Winnemucca

Higher education opportunities in the 19th century slowly began to open for women. Native American Sarah Winnemucca was a remarkable woman who was able to successfully bridge the culture of her people and that of the European settlers. Because of her dedication and work, a better understanding was achieved between the two cultures.

Born to an influential Paiute family near Humboldt, Nevada, in 1844, Sarah Winnemucca's Paiute name was Thocmentony, which translates to Shell Flower. The daughter of Chief Winnemucca and the granddaughter of Chief Truckee, Sarah Winnemucca was highly educated and persevered in a time when women, especially Native American women, faced many obstacles.

Aside from her work as an interpreter in the Bureau of Indian Affairs at Fort McDermitt, she was an activist, lecturer, educator, and advocate for the rights of Native Americans. As an educator, she opened a school for Native American children in Lovelock to teach Paiute language and culture.

A Well Deserved Honor

In 1993, Sarah Winnemucca was honored with a posthumous induction into the Nevada Writers Hall of Fame. In 2005, the state of Nevada contributed a statue of her by sculptor Benjamin Victor to the National Statuary Hall Collection in the US Capitol, a fitting honor indeed to a woman who strove to see that her people were not overlooked or forgotten as non-native peoples continued their western migration.

Her 1883 book, *Life Among the Paiutes: Their Wrongs and Claims,* focused attention on the plight of Native Americans and is considered to be the first known autobiography written by a Native American woman.

Charlie Chaplin's Leading Lady

Nevada boasts many museums, big and small. If you're a Charlie Chaplin fan and silent-era film buff, you're in for a special treat at the Humboldt County Museum in Winnemucca. Here you will discover memorabilia of silent-screen actress Edna Purviance who costarred with Charlie Chaplin in 34 of his films. And Edna happened to be a Nevada girl. On display at the museum are photos of Edna, one of the dresses she is said to have worn in the 1917 short comedy film *The Adventurer*, several Charlie Chaplin dolls, and more.

The youngest of three children, Edna Purviance was born in Paradise Valley on October 21, 1895. The family moved to Lovelock when Edna was a small child. After graduating from Lovelock High School, Edna moved to San Francisco with an older sister. There she studied stenography and worked as an office clerk. She may have wound up being an obscure office manager if

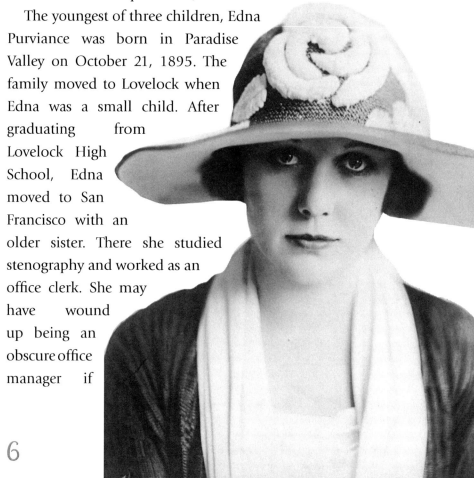

not for Charlie Chaplin, who took one look at her and realized she was the actress he'd been looking for. But could she act? After spending some time with her, Chaplin was certain she could pull it off and wasted little time offering her a costarring role in one of his films.

Edna was speechless. She had come to San Francisco for excitement, and here she was being offered a job as an actress. In comparison, stenography and office work seemed dull; she was ready for adventure and readily agreed to accompany him back to Los Angeles.

Their first film together was *A Night Out* in 1915. Edna proved to be the perfect costar for Charlie. They kept themselves busy that first year, cranking out several other films, including the Chaplin classic *The Tramp*. Eventually, a romance ensued. Life was fun for the young lovers.

He Never Forgot

Actress Edna Purviance achieved fame during the early days of movies, and yet she was all but forgotten in her home state of Nevada. However, Charlie Chaplin never forgot her. After their romance ended, they remained good friends. Chaplin would continue in the movie industry for many years, while Edna made two films in 1927 and retired shortly afterward, although she did have a small uncredited part in two of Chaplin's films: 1947's *Monsieur Verdoux* and 1952's *Limelight*. Chaplin and Purviance never married, but he assured that she would never go without by keeping her on his film company's payroll until her death on January 13, 1958.

Nevada's Politicians

Politics make strange bedfellows . . . so said essayist Charles Dudley Warner in 1870. Things haven't changed much since then. No US president has come from Nevada (yet). But Nevada has bragging rights to a first lady. Patricia (Thelma Catherine "Pat" Ryan) Nixon, wife of Richard Milhous "I'm-not-a-crook" Nixon, was born right here in the Silver State. Born in Ely on March 16, 1912, Patricia was a toddler when the family moved to Southern California. Nonetheless, Nevada holds onto its first lady claim.

Ronald ("What-Would-Reagan-Do?") Reagan may not have come from Nevada, but he holds the distinction of being the only US president to ever perform in a Las Vegas showroom (yet). It was 1954, and his career as an entertainer was on the skids. Reagan took a job at the New Frontier, where the future president of the United States acted as the frontman for a group of chimpanzees and showgirls. He needed money, and he had a name. The show flopped. His political career did not. The rest is history. Hail to the Chief!

In 1960, newly elected president John F. Kennedy found himself with a strong Hollywood connection by way of his brother-in-law, actor Peter Lawford. Lawford was a member of the Rat Pack, a suave group of male entertainers who embodied the sophistication of the early 1960s. The Rat Pack included Frank Sinatra, Dean Martin, Joey Bishop, and Sammy Davis Jr. All of them were impressed with the White House connection, especially Frank Sinatra, who had recently purchased the Cal Neva Lodge at Crystal Bay.

There's no telling how far the friendship might have gone if Sinatra hadn't permitted mafia member Sam Giancana to

Friends in High Places

It wasn't a done deal when Frank Sinatra lost his Nevada gaming license in 1963 for permitting mobster Sam Giancana into his gaming establishment, the Cal Neva at Crystal Bay Lake Tahoe. JFK might have snubbed him, but Sinatra realized that it pays to have friends in high places. Eighteen years later, Sinatra sought another gaming license from the state of Nevada. With a character witness like then-President Ronald Reagan, how could he go wrong? He couldn't. And he was praised for his charitable work and even awarded a gaming license in 1981 for his job as an entertainment public relations consultant for the Caesar's Palace Hotel Casino.

visit the Cal Neva. Giancana was listed in the Nevada Gaming Commission's black book of people never allowed within Nevada casinos. When it was discovered, Sinatra fought with the gaming commission, losing his gaming license and, ultimately, the Cal Neva. According to one story, John Kennedy was visiting Las Vegas and riding with Governor Grant Sawyer when he commented on how hard Nevada was being on Frank Sinatra. Governor Sawyer ignored the comment, and Kennedy said no more. But his friendship with Sinatra was over.

An old postcard showing Ronald Reagan
in a Las Vegas showroom

9

Hizzoner, the Mayor

Before we leave the politicians to their photo ops, tax increases, and campaign promises, let's take a look at two Nevada mayors who helped shape their cities. As a defense attorney, former Las Vegas Mayor Oscar Goodman counted among his clients mob enforcer Tony "The Ant" Spilotro. Spilotro, you may recall, had the misfortune of meeting the wrong people in an Indiana cornfield.

Oscar Goodman is a colorful character who holds some strong opinions, and he isn't the least bit shy about sharing them. As mayor, the flamboyant Goodman continually strove to keep his city in the forefront and garnered worldwide attention for Las Vegas more than once.

But Goodman was not the first Nevada mayor to have thrust the city he presided over into the spotlight.

Long before Oscar Goodman was born, Reno's colorful mayor Edwin E. Roberts was focusing attention on his city for his opinion on the merits of prohibition. In his opposition to the Volstead Act, Roberts was a man ahead of his time.

Edwin E. Roberts

A Man of His Time

For all his modern ideas, E. E. Roberts had one blind spot. He did not like gambling, nor did he see the tourists it would bring or the financial boon it would be to Reno and the Silver State. Nevada legalized gambling in 1931, the same year that Roberts won reelection as Reno's mayor.

Prohibition might be the law of the land, but to the delight of news reporters across the globe, Roberts openly declared it a joke.

In 1931, he was running for reelection to his third term of office as Reno's mayor. When Dr. Case, pastor of the Reno Methodist Church, invited him and his two opponents to speak at the church, Roberts gladly accepted; his opponents declined. On March

Oscar Goodman, courtesy of Gage Skidmore

29, E. E. Roberts addressed his audience from the pulpit. He took exception with recent remarks made by Dr. Clarence True Wilson, director of the Methodist Board of Temperance Prohibition and Public Morals. Dr. Wilson had declared Reno to be a combination of "Sodom, Gomorrah and Hell."

While Roberts agreed that Reno had its share of corruption, he pointed out that the city also had plenty of churches and fine schools. His words concerning prohibition were quoted in newspapers around the globe and have been quoted ever since.

"If I had my way, I'd place a barrel of whiskey on every corner, with a dipper and a sign saying, 'Help yourself but don't be a hog.' I've been trying to make Reno a place where everybody can do as they please, just as long as they don't interfere with other people's rights."

Mark Twain

Samuel Clemens was born in Hannibal, Missouri, on November 30, 1835, but as you'll soon see, Mark Twain was born in Nevada. It might never have been if President Abraham Lincoln hadn't sent Orion Clemens, older brother of Samuel, west to act as

secretary of the Nevada Territory. It all seemed like such an adventure that Samuel asked his brother if he might accompany him on the journey. And we all know that Orion said yes.

When they arrived in Carson City on August 14, 1861, Orion went about his work in politics, and Samuel was left to his own devices. He first tried mining. The work was grueling and unrewarding and didn't suit young Clemens. After a series of letters written to the *Territorial Enterprise*, Samuel Clemens was offered a job as a writer at the newspaper. Finally, Clemens had found a job and a town (Virginia City) that suited him. When the brash Clemens wasn't writing outlandish articles for the *Territorial Enterprise*, he was hanging out at one of the local saloons. It was either in Virginia City or Carson City, depending on which city you ask, where Samuel Clemens took the pen name Mark Twain.

Twain didn't stay in Virginia City but just a few years. According to one story, he jokingly challenged a competing newspaper editor to a duel, and realizing his mistake, he hastily beat it out of town before the law could catch up with him; dueling was outlawed in Nevada. Another story holds that it was the newspaper editor who challenged Twain to the duel. Either way, Mark Twain left Nevada for California.

Twain Was Born in Nevada

Samuel Clemens has achieved legend status in Nevada, although he only lived in the Silver State for two years. During those years, Clemens began his writing career at the *Territorial Enterprise* in Virginia City and took the *nom de plume* Mark Twain. It was here that he developed his wry writing style, some believe because of his association with Dan De Quille (William Wright), who was a writer at the newspaper as well. Twain wrote at least 28 books; one of his all-time favorites with readers is his 1872 book, *Roughing It*. The book covers incidents from his trip westward with his brother Orion and from his travels in the west and tells some colorful tales of his time in Virginia City.

Rafael Rivera: The Man Who Named Las Vegas

About the time the Declaration of Independence was being signed, Spanish missionaries were looking for a route between their missions in Arizona and those in California; they first entered present-day southern Nevada sometime around 1776. The route they carved out would be known as the Spanish Trail.

Fifty years later in 1830, Antonio Armijo's party of traders was traveling along the trail when Mexican scout Rafael Rivera decided to take a shortcut.

In doing so he became the first non–Native American to come into the Las Vegas Valley. Looking at Las Vegas's sprawl today, it is hard to imagine the breathtaking sight Rivera was rewarded with. Before him were lush, verdant natural springs

More Than Bright Lights and Gaming

Springs Preserve is the best bang-for-the-family-buck that Las Vegas has to offer. Known as the birthplace of Las Vegas, Springs Preserve is believed to be where Rafael Rivera first came into the Las Vegas valley. Springs Preserve is an enjoyable place for the entire family with its gardens, butterfly habitat, museum, and more. Eat at the café or pack a picnic and plan to spend the day. Either way, be sure to wear comfortable shoes, as there is much to see and do here while learning more about this region. Free landscaping classes and lectures are offered here, as well as the not-to-be-missed annual Earth Day festival.

that seemed to glitter in the scorching sun. Word quickly spread of the welcoming oasis with its cool relief from the hostile desert environment; soon, others would find their way to the natural springs. Rafael Rivera would call this place Las Vegas, which is Spanish for "the meadows." And the place still glitters to this day, but decidedly in a more spectacular and different way than when Rafael Rivera first laid eyes on it.

Rafael Rivera statue in Las Vegas

The Mysterious Queho

Queho didn't know his parents. His mother died shortly after giving birth to him, and the identity of his father remains a mystery. Raised by his mother's relatives at the reservation in Las Vegas, he was not accepted by the others because of a deformity. In the superstitious world in which he lived, any kind of deformity

Queho's skeleton and the posse who chased him

was looked at as a bad omen. Some say it was Queho's club foot that made him an outcast. Others believe his right leg was noticeably shorter than his left. Regardless, this served to see that Queho was unloved and unwanted. Consequently, he grew up resentful and suspicious of almost everyone he encountered.

Legend has it that Queho turned to the same crimes as his step-brother outlaw, Paiute Avote. Some believe he was responsible for the deaths of at least 23 men. Robbery and pillaging were also part of his criminal repertoire. An altogether bad hombre, Queho had to be stopped. But how were they going to do this when no one knew their way around the canyon better than Queho? Lawmen came looking for him but always left empty-handed. After committing a crime, Queho would take refuge in the rocks and caves. He could always wait them out.

Eventually, the lawmen who had chased him gave up on ever finding him. They grew old, and they died, but there was still

Eat Your Heart Out, Paul Revere

How was Queho able to ride in the Las Vegas Helldorado Days parade years after his death? Once the discovery of outlaw Queho's remains was announced, everyone was curious to take a look at his remains. Strange as it sounds today, a squabble over who held ownership of the remains ensued. In fact, it would be years before Queho was afforded a proper burial. Before that time, the remains were used by different Las Vegas groups and were displayed during Helldorado Days. In 1975, Roland Wiley, a former Las Vegas attorney, secured the remains and buried Queho at Wiley's Pahrump Valley Ranch.

no sign of Queho. Many stories were told around Las Vegas; Queho was long gone and living far from the area. He walked the streets of Las Vegas, big as you please. Some even suspected that Queho's ghost hovered over the canyon, taunting all those who had ever chased him. It seemed that there was a different tale for every day of the week. Then one day in 1940, the mystery was solved.

One morning three prospectors were working along a steep cliff high above the Colorado River in the Black Rock Canyon. One of the men discovered a low stonewall near a spot some 2,000 feet above the river. Thinking that this would make the perfect hideout, he gazed down into the canyon far below. From this vantage point, a man would be able to see in all directions. He called to his friends, who came running. As the three men explored farther, they discovered a small cave with a trip wire running across it. Why on earth, they wondered, would someone set up a crude alarm system at the cave's entrance? Looking farther into the cave, they discovered the skeletal remains of Queho. He might have escaped the lawmen, but he couldn't escape fate.

Anne Henrietta Martin

Anne Henrietta Martin was a history professor who established the history department at her alma mater, the University of Nevada Reno (UNR), in 1897.

Anne Henrietta Martin was also an early-day suffragette who fought tirelessly for Nevada's women's rights. Between 1912 and 1914, she traveled the state, stopping to speak in every county for Nevada's women's right to vote. In 1917, Martin, as a member of the women's rights group Silent Sentinels traveled to Washington, DC, to picket for women's suffrage in front of the White House on July 14, 1917. She, along with hundreds of other women, was arrested for obstructing traffic and sentenced to jail. A week later, President Woodrow Wilson pardoned the women.

Undeterred, Martin continued her work with the suffragette movement. In 1918 and again in 1920, she became the first woman to run for US Senate from Nevada. She ran as an independent and lost both elections.

From Anne Henrietta Martin's 1919 article in *Good Housekeeping* magazine:

The question we must have answered in the coming campaign is not "What shall women do for the political parties?" but "What shall the political parties do for women?"

Aside from her writing and her passion for women's rights, Anne Martin served as president of the Nevada Women's Civic League and was Nevada's first woman tennis champion.

Eilley Bowers

No other woman in Nevada's history has been written about more than Eilley Bowers. Eilley's self-proclaimed ability to communicate with the spirit world may have helped create her legend. But it was her marriage to Comstock miner Sandy Bowers that guaranteed Eilley's place in Nevada's history.

Her marriage to Sandy Bowers seemed to be the beginning of a rags-to-riches and happily-ever-after life. Sandy Bowers had just struck it rich at his mining claim. The bride and groom were the wealthiest miners in Virginia City. Sandy even made the remark that they had money "to throw at the birds."

And they did. The Bowerses traveled across Europe, spending lavishly on furnishings and decor for their mansion that was being built in nearby Washoe Valley. Tragedy struck when they returned home; Sandy died of pneumonia, leaving Eilley alone and penniless. Sandy hadn't been the sharp businessman she believed him to be.

Did She Stay On?

Eilley Bowers may have gone from rags to riches to rags again, but all was not lost. She would no doubt be thrilled to know that her beloved Bowers Mansion is today a popular spot with tourists and locals alike who enjoy touring the home of Nevada's two early-day millionaires. After seeing Bowers Mansion, many choose to stroll the grounds or relax under tall trees while picnicking. Some may even contemplate the ghostly legends associated with Bowers Mansion. Sightings of Eilley, who is said to walk the grounds during the early morning hours, have been reported for many years by passing motorists.

After losing her mansion and all her fine furnishings to creditors, Eilley was forced to live by her wits. In her homeland of Scotland, women had been seeking guidance through their peep stones (crystal ball) for centuries. Eilley began offering her services as a seer (fortune teller/medium) to those in need of help from beyond.

She may have suffered some ridicule for this, but it put food on her table. Her ability as an accurate fortune teller brought new clients her way, even if people like Dan De Quille (William Wright) poked a bit of fun at her in his book *Big Bonanza*.

She died in 1903 and is buried near her beloved Sandy on the little hill overlooking Bowers Mansion. Yes, it's still there in Washoe Valley. And worth a trip to see how a 19th-century silver magnate lived.

Howard Hughes

Reclusive billionaire Howard Hughes reshaped Nevada's gaming industry in the late 1960s and early '70s with his purchases of several Las Vegas and then Reno hotels/casinos. Living in Hollywood, Hughes was well aware that Las Vegas was just a hop, skip, and jump away—or, in his case, an easy flight.

Flying was his passion, but not all flights ended smoothly. On May 17, 1943, Hughes was testing his amphibious aircraft, the Sikorsky S-43, at Lake Mead when it crashed into the lake, killing two of his passengers. He recuperated for a time at the Boulder Hotel in Boulder City. This may have been his first serious look at the possibilities of Las Vegas.

In 1957, Hughes married actress Jean Peters in a secret ceremony in Tonopah, a little town located halfway between Las Vegas and Reno. Some say it was at the haunted Mizpah Hotel that the lovebirds exchanged vows; others say it was at an old motel that was razed years ago. The marriage sent Peters into retirement and Hughes into a buying frenzy of Nevada properties. In 1968, he bought the Silver Slipper in Las Vegas. Rumor has it that while spending the night at another place, he was so annoyed with

A Penny for Your Thoughts, a Million for a Ride

A disheveled Howard Hughes figures in a story told by Melvin Dummar. Dummar claimed to have picked up the hitchhiker (Hughes) in the Nevada desert near Lida Junction on Highway 95 one night in 1967, about 150 miles north of Las Vegas. According to Dummar, Hughes was so grateful for the ride that he later wrote a will leaving 1/16 of his fortune to him. Called the Mormon Will, it was found to be a forgery in 1978 by a Las Vegas jury. Some say it's possible that Dummar gave Hughes a ride from Lida Junction to the Sands in Las Vegas, but highly unlikely that he left him $156 million for his kindness. That works out to be over a million dollars a mile—and that would be a very expensive ride, indeed.

the rooftop spinning-slipper display that he bought the casino just so he could take the lighted slipper down. It only cost him $5.4 million dollars to do so. But what was money to someone like Howard Hughes?

Next up, he bought the Frontier and the Desert Inn. The lore attached to this purchase has Hughes and his employees staying in the penthouse. When management asked him to leave, Hughes refused. But they needed the penthouse for high rollers (big-money gamblers). Hughes settled the argument by purchasing the Desert Inn.

How, you may wonder, did Hughes change Nevada gaming? He ushered in the corporate casino industry and displaced the small, family-run establishments of the past.

Washoe Club

Chapter Two

Paranormal Nevada

If your journey into Nevada includes ghosts, hauntings, and things that go bump in the night, take note. Aside from being home to the most acclaimed ghost investigator in the United States, Zak Bagans, Nevada also lays claim to some of the most haunted hot spots in the country.

. . . .

Virginia City

Several years ago, Zak Bagans proclaimed the tiny town of Virginia City to be the Disneyland of Ghost hunters. He was correct. There are probably more ghosts per square foot here in Virginia City than there is sagebrush in the desert. And that's almost the truth. One of the ghosts said to wander the boardwalk is that of Mark Twain, who lived in Virginia City for a short time before moving on to literary greatness.

Virginia City was founded in 1859 by those who'd come up to this spot on the side of Mt. Davidson, seeking wealth through the discovery of silver. Some of them, like John Mackay, struck it rich beyond their wildest dreams. Others weren't so lucky. Many of these men and women rest in the Silver Terrace Cemetery on the edge of town. And just so you know, there are more residents in the cemetery than in the town. That's okay.

Thank You, President Lincoln

Nevada's silver helped to turn the tide of the Civil War. Before the discovery of silver, migrants traveling westward didn't stop and put down roots in what we know today as Nevada. Most of the land was barren and dry desert. There was nothing remarkable here, and there weren't a lot of resources such as water, plants, and vegetation either. All that changed with the 1859 announcement of the discovery of silver in Virginia City. Known as the Comstock Lode, this was the first major discovery of silver in the United States. President Abraham Lincoln noticed and was instrumental in seeing that Nevada attained statehood.

Ghosts occasionally wander in and out of the old buildings that line C Street—just looking for a friendly ghost hunter.

Ghosts don't wait for the Halloween season to appear. They are year-round here in Virginia City. Ask in any saloon, hotel, or other business. They'll surely share a ghost tale or two with you.

The Washoe Club

Ask anyone involved in the paranormal. The Washoe Club in Virginia City is numero uno when it comes to ghost hunting. This is home, the place where ghost hunters come to party, to fete, and to memorialize those who've gone on to the next world. For a pithy membership fee of $25, ghost hunters and others are permitted to use the members' room, tour the museum with some fine paranormal displays, and enjoy a half-price drink night once a year.

Some excellent evidence of ghosts has been captured in the upstairs ballroom area. This is stuff like electronic voice phenomena (EVP) and video. And let's not forget that this is the location where Zak and his team on *Ghost Adventures* first captured a full-body apparition on video. But Zak isn't the only one. Many people who've visited the Washoe Club have had experiences with ghosts. Women are sometimes locked in the bathroom;

Ghosts Are Everywhere

The Washoe Club is a historic old saloon where locals love to gather for a drink and a good time. Ghost investigators come here for the very same reason. It's all subjective. What's your idea of a good time? If you are thrilled at the idea of hanging out at a historic location where ghosts tread and are always ready and hoping for a ghostly encounter, read on. But one thing we know about ghosts is that they don't always appear when we want them to. So how will we know that a haunted location is really haunted? It isn't always about seeing a ghost. The amount of evidence gathered by ghost investigators at a certain location is a good indicator. In Virginia City, the Washoe Club is the location where a lot of evidence is being captured by many different people at different times of the day and night.

some people have been grabbed or touched. If the thought of hanging out in the dark with ghosts doesn't scare you, think of this—for a fee, you and your team can book the place and investigate all night long. Who knows what, or who, you might encounter?

Goldfield Hotel

What is it about old hotels and ghosts? Perhaps it is the solitude that such places afford; then again, it may be memories of times long gone. Whatever their reasons, ghosts seem to enjoy their stay here at the Goldfield Hotel—there is no checkout time; they are welcome to stay as long as they like.

The Goldfield Hotel in Goldfield is probably on every ghost hunter's bucket list of places to investigate. And there's a good reason for this. The place is eerie and haunted. I'll just add an FYI here: not all the ghosts that hang out here in the old has-been hotel are the friendly sort. You're on their turf, and they don't always like it. Ghosts have been known to punch, pinch, kick, and curse people in the hotel during late-night hours.

Ghost-hunting TV shows have come to the hotel and endured some strange experiences in the process. One star of a popular show was possessed by a decidedly mean ghost. Another was threatened and called vile names. An early TV show got away lightly in comparison. Their biggest mishap was that every piece of equipment on the shoot stopped working at the same time. Was it the ghosts? They believed so. And after apologies all around, the equipment was once again functional.

Legend has it that a young woman was chained to a radiator and left to die in Room 109 of the hotel way back in the day. Ghost hunters have reported several encounters with the unfortunate woman over the years. Then, too, there is the woman who spritzes everyone she encounters with lilac perfume, the ghostly cowboy who'd just as soon pick you up and toss you as to look at you, and the ghostly businessman whose trail of cigar smoke is a dead giveaway of his presence. No pun intended.

Virgil Earp, Lawman

Goldfield is a small town with a big history. At the turn of the 20th century, Goldfield was where all the state's movers and shakers lived. It also happened to be Nevada's largest town. That's hard to believe when we consider Las Vegas some 250 miles south down Highway 95. But it's a fact. And so is the fact that Virgil Earp (Wyatt's older brother) was a deputy sheriff here in Goldfield. The old lawman contracted pneumonia and died here with his boots off in 1905. But don't look for Virgil's grave at the Goldfield Cemetery—he isn't there. He's buried in Oregon. Some have said that his ghost occasionally makes an appearance at the site of his death. He is just one of many of Goldfield's ghosts.

Miss Dana's Tea Shoppe and the Eureka Tunnels

Eureka is a small mining town in Eastern Nevada with a rich mining history and some very friendly residents. You don't want to visit Eureka without stopping in at Miss Dana's Tea Shoppe. Miss Dana is Dana Freund, Eureka's tourism director; she knows where all the fun happens, where the history takes place, and where the ghosts hang out.

Surprisingly, there are many different haunted locations for the ghost hunter to explore in this small town. One that is truly amazing is the tunnels located beneath the Afterlife Antiques and Oddities Store, which happens to be right next door to Miss Dana's Tea Shoppe.

The tunnels were built by Chinese laborers, and some who investigated claims that a few of their ghosts are still working in the tunnel. No one who has investigated the tunnels has come

Haunted Family Fun

Ghost walks are a fun way for the whole family to learn about a location's history and ghosts. They are popular tourist attractions everywhere you go. Aficionados of ghost walks should know that Dana Freund presents one of the best ghost walks I've ever had the pleasure of being on. Miss Dana has a charming personality that makes the foray into the dark night streets of Eureka fun, informative, and eerie. Don't say boo; Miss Dana will even show you how to capture some ghostly evidence with your cell phone if you like.

away without some amazing evidence of ghostly activity. And that's a fact.

Now, have Miss Dana pour you a cup of apple cider tea and show you the correct way to stir your tea. Yes, my friend, there is a right way and a wrong way to stir tea.

Zak Bagans's Haunted Museum

If you're looking for something a bit different from the extravaganza showroom presentations on the Strip, consider a museum. Not just any museum, but a museum that is far different from those of a school field trip museum. Are you thinking macabre? Good, then you get the idea. And who better to do such a museum than spooky TV star Zak Bagans?

What do you do if you've got one of television's most popular ghost-hunting shows? If you are Zak Bagans, you indulge your

passion for the paranormal by opening up your own Haunted Museum. And that's just what Zak did on April 2, 2016. He's been collecting oddities and macabre memorabilia for many years and shares it all with the world at the Haunted Museum on Charleston Boulevard.

Regardless of the season, expect a crowd. This is one of the hottest attractions in Las Vegas. Expect to see things that you aren't going to see anywhere else in the universe. Haunted dolls, Dr. (Death) Kevorkian's van, and the personal effects of cold-blooded killers are among the items on display. Gruesome, perhaps; it's certainly not everyone's cup of tea. But it is one of the most popular tourist attractions in Las Vegas.

And there are ghosts. Some people who've visited have experienced ghostly activity while touring the museum. But what do you expect? This is the Haunted Museum, after all.

Chapter Three

Nevada Out of This World

It could be said Nevada is a place that extraterrestrials prefer to visit. But then again, Nevada is a state with a lot of wide-open spaces, a state with plenty of night sky that doesn't suffer light pollution. No wonder there are numerous UFO sightings here in the Silver State.

Nellis Air Force Base

In 1940, the US Army Corps of Engineers began a search for a suitable location for its flexible aerial gunnery school. Several areas in Nevada, Arizona, and Utah were up for consideration.

Nevada won out. And Las Vegas was chosen because of its nearly perfect flying weather and its terrain. Besides that, the price was right. At a dollar per acre price, the public domain land was ideal. Originally named Las Vegas Air Force Base, the name was later changed to honor William Harrell Nellis, who was killed in action during World War II.

Only about eight miles from downtown Las Vegas, Nellis covers more than two million acres and is known as the Home of the Fighter Pilot. It is also known as a place with plenty of secrets. Located deep within the confines of Nellis Air Force

Courtesy of Glen Highcove, Dreamstime.com

Base is the mysterious Area 51 Groom Lake. Only authorized personnel are permitted access. The compound is impenetrable; any place off-site that might afford a view belongs to the federal government and is also off-limits. Warning signs are clearly posted, and armed guards reconnoiter the entire area. Trespassers will always be arrested. No excuses; no exceptions.

Why all this secrecy, you ask? UFOs, captive aliens, and secret experiments are rumored to be the reason for the government's diligence at keeping people out.

These aren't the only strange goings-on that happen here at Nellis Air Force Base.

Of Atomic Bombs

Roughly 84.5 percent of Nevada's land is owned and controlled by the US government. Much of that land is used for military purposes as highly secure, secret facilities. Ever heard of Area 51? How about Dreamland? Stories are numerous; one has the US government housing extraterrestrials at the facility. In another tale, UFOs regularly fly in and around this area. Scan the sky all you want. But don't go snooping beyond the posted signs; you will run afoul of the US government.

In the late 1980s, a Las Vegas television station interviewed a man who claimed to have worked on alien spacecraft. The public was intrigued and wanted to know more. The government was tight-lipped. This only fueled curiosity.

It all started after World War II. The United States wanted to stay on top of this new and powerful warfare. For this purpose, President Harry S. Truman approved the establishment of the Nevada Proving Grounds in 1951. This 680-square-mile area in the Nevada desert, known as Yucca Flats, had first been selected by the Atomic Energy Commission for its remoteness. Located 65 miles northwest of Las Vegas, no one realized that one day the Las Vegas area would be Nevada's most densely populated, with over a million people.

But that was decades down the highway when the first atmospheric test was conducted at the facility. Eleven nuclear tests were carried out in 1953. In May of that year, a powerful 32-kiloton atomic bomb was detonated as part of Operation Upshot Knothole. For the next 40 years, more than 900 atomic tests would be conducted. One hundred of these were above ground. The proving grounds area was nearly doubled to 1,350

square miles. And the United States Department of Energy installation was renamed the Nevada Test Site (NTS).

In nearby Las Vegas, there were celebrations of the resulting mushroom clouds with hairstyles, casino contests, and giveaways. Families living nearby were encouraged to sit outside and watch the mushroom clouds. No one realized the danger as the wind swept across the Nevada desert in a northeasterly direction toward St. George, Utah, and the surrounding area.

The Conqueror and the Red Sand

So, now you know that if you've never watched *The Conqueror* on late-night TV, you haven't missed anything. The film was a box-office disaster even though it starred two of Hollywood's top stars, John Wayne as Genghis Khan and Susan Hayward as Princess Bortai. While the 1956 film was a flop, it would, in time, bring awareness of the dangers of atomic testing in Nevada.

Two hundred cast and crew members, including John Wayne, Susan Hayward, Dick Powell, and Agnes Moorehead, filmed scenes in the red sand of Snow Canyon in Utah's St. George area. When the location shooting was finished, they returned to Hollywood to complete the film. But producer Howard Hughes was a stickler for realism. Hughes reasoned that since the film was being shot in Technicolor, he would have to make sure that the colors matched. To achieve this, he had 60 tons of the red sand shipped to the soundstage in Hollywood. There were top-notch stars and great publicity, but nothing could save the film; *The Conqueror* was voted one of the worst movies of the 1950s. The film was panned and quickly forgotten.

Duke in the Desert without His Six Shooter

In what film did "The Duke," aka John Wayne, play Genghis Khan? That question is sure to stump some of your film-buff pals. Who can imagine the plain-spoken cowpoke as Khan? Apparently, someone in Hollywood did. And that's how Wayne came to star in the box office disaster *The Conqueror*. An adventure love story of sorts with Princess Bortai (Susan Hayward) falling for Genghis Khan (John Wayne), the movie is bad—so bad that it was named as possibly one of the worst films ever made.

And then . . . some of those who worked on the film began dying of cancer. Of the 220 people that worked on the film, 91 were diagnosed with cancer. Was the red sand contaminated with deadly radioactive fallout the winds had brought northward to Utah from the Nevada test site?

A 1980 article in *People* magazine pointed out that 91 of 220 have been diagnosed with cancer was an off-the-chart high 41 percent morbidity rate. At the article's writing, half of the 91 had already died as a result of cancer, including stars John Wayne and Susan Hayward. While it is true that many of these people were smokers, it is believed their deaths were the result of fallout from Nevada testing.

Ely's UFO Crash Site

Flying saucers were all the rage in the mid-20th century. What was out there? Movies about creatures visiting from other galaxies hit the theaters, and stories about sightings were regular newspaper items. On June 28, 1950, the *Reno Evening Gazette* carried a story about Ely. It seemed that hundreds of the town's residents had reported seeing something strange in the night sky. The object was described as spiraling smoke that could have been a falling airplane or . . . a flying saucer. Reports of flying saucers or UFOs were common throughout Nevada.

Two years later on August 8, 1952, another story appeared in the *Reno Evening Gazette* concerning flying saucers. But some newspapers were tired of such stories. The Ottawa, Illinois, *Daily Republican-Times* didn't like all the saucer sightings being reported and decided it would no longer "feed such pap" to its readers. In refusing to carry stories about strange objects in the sky, the newspaper invited thousands of other newspapers across the nation to join it in denying space to saucer stories.

Be Careful What You Wish For

The story of a crashed UFO and dead space aliens made Roswell, New Mexico, a household name. Unfortunately, this didn't happen with Ely's UFO crash incident. The story was shared across the United States and soon forgotten by everyone but the locals. Still, some Ely residents continued to watch the sky in hopes that one night a UFO might once again appear.

They didn't. And stories of mysterious glowing objects that raced across Nevada's skies continued to appear in print. Still, not all saucer stories made the news.

According to an Ely tale, a young woman was entertaining dinner guests on an August evening in 1952 when she happened to look out at the horizon. She couldn't believe her eyes as a flying saucer crashed to earth. Those who were first on the scene soon realized that the strange craft was not of this earth and that all of its occupants were dead. Apparently, the space travelers had been killed on impact.

Some insisted that before anything else could be learned, the government (as it is wont to do) sent a highly secret team to confiscate what was left of the strange vehicle and all 16 bodies of the space aliens onboard.

Courtesy of Bill Oberding

Flying Saucers over the Biggest Little City... and Beyond

One spring night in 1950, something very strange reportedly happened in the skies over Reno. Several people at the Mapes Hotel Skyroom in downtown looked out into the sky and saw flying saucers to the south. According to the *Reno Evening Gazette*, there were at least six or seven of the objects that appeared rounded with windows from which shone red and green lights. The unusual craft hovered over the hospital and the airfield before speeding into the distance. Witnesses insisted that whatever the flying objects were, they were definitely not airplanes.

Courtesy of gchapel, iStock

Two years later, three people were traveling from Reno to Winnemucca when they noticed silvery discs in the early evening sky. The driver pulled to the side of the roadway, and the three observers counted not one, not two—but 22 silvery flying saucers hovering motionless in the sky. The saucers sped away, disappearing into the night sky. And after promising each other to make a full report to the local newspaper, they drove on across the desert.

Fifteen years later near the same vicinity, three miners reported seeing something strange in the sky. According to the witnesses, the object in question was honeycomb shaped with glowing lights on the inside. Although the craft seemed to have windows, they were unable to see anyone inside. Nervous about the whole thing, the miners kept their distance from the UFO that appeared to be observing them. Suddenly, as they watched, the craft went straight up in the air and sped away.

Extraterrestrial Highway

If the state of Nevada knows anything, it's how to capitalize on opportunity. As an example, the renaming of State Route 375, the roadway with the most reported UFO sightings in the state. State Assemblyman Roy Neighbors thought he had a great idea when he introduced a bill to officially rename State Route 375 to the Extraterrestrial Alien Highway. The assembly agreed and passed Neighbors's bill. But the bill was killed in the senate.

Changing highway signs and markers would not only be costly but frivolous as well. The debate raged on. In April 1996, State Route 375 was officially declared the Extraterrestrial Highway by Nevada Governor Bob Miller, officiating over the ceremonies that included other Nevada dignitaries and actors from the film *Independence Day*.

Driving the Extraterrestrial Highway during daylight is a lonely proposition. After dark, this lonely stretch of highway gets dangerous as it winds its way across the Tikaboo, Sand Spring, and Railroad Valleys. Not because of UFOs that might teleport you up to a nearby spacecraft, but because of the open range (as in no fences) and the cattle that might wander onto the highway. That's something to think about while scanning the night's skies.

If you find yourself wondering what secrets lie behind those locked gates, stop and remember that Area 51 (aka Dreamland,) is a top-secret air force facility. It's a facility in which no one except those with special top governmental clearance is permitted entrance. Look around. Armed guards are continually on patrol, making sure would-be trespassers stay out.

Should you be caught crossing into the restricted area by accident or intention, you will be detained at gunpoint. The Lincoln County Sheriff will come and arrest you, and you'll be slapped with a heavy fine.

Top Secret Stay Away

What secrets are hidden behind the gates at Area 51? Some believe that secret weapons and aircraft are being developed and tested there. Another story that's been told forever (or at least a very long time) involves the bodies of dead space travelers and their craft being kept behind lock and key. One thing is certain. You should obey all signs and stay away from the restricted area or wish you had . . . don't say I didn't warn you.

Little A'le'Inn in Rachel

If you're seeking UFOs, conspiracy theories, and tales of men in black, be sure to check out the only business in town, the Little A'le'Inn in Rachel, the only town on the Extraterrestrial Highway. After all, this is the UFO Capital of the World. Little A'le'Inn is a friendly, down-home bar/café with rooms to rent. If you aren't expecting four-star accommodations and don't mind sharing a single-wide mobile home with other lodgers, you're in luck.

The food's good, the people who live here are friendly, and sooner or later, the talk turns to UFOs; everyone's got something to say on the subject. Shopaholics take note: yes, even out here in the middle of the Nevada desert,

Courtesy of Robert Michaud, iStock

What's in a Name?

Aside from UFOs, the number one question asked around here is, how did Rachel get its name? Originally called Tempiute Village, then Sand Springs, the town was named Rachel after Rachel Jones, the first and only baby born in the valley. Rachel Jones's family moved to Washington State a short time later. Sadly, the little girl died there at the age of three.

While scanning the skies for UFOs, keep in mind that this is an area of open range. Cattle are not fenced in and roam freely.

there are lots of souvenirs, books on the subject of aliens, and other products to buy.

Rachel is in the middle of nowhere, but don't expect a lot of peace and quiet. Very near the Nellis Range Complex, the town is subjected to many loud sonic booms because of all the military exercises in the area. Rachel is new as far as towns go. Founded in 1973, the tiny town of Rachel is about 100 miles north of Las Vegas and has just as many (98) residents. Rachel bills itself as being located on the *World's Only Extraterrestrial Highway*. Remember to fill your gas tank before heading this way. The gas station in Rachel is (at this writing) closed. The nearest gas is 50 miles away in Ash Springs.

Courtesy of iStock

The Mysterious McDermitt Lights

What are the mysterious lights that have been seen around McDermitt for nearly a hundred years? Anyone who has witnessed the strange phenomena has a theory, but no one knows for sure. The McDermitt Lights were first written about in the very first issue of *Fate* magazine way back in 1948. The author of that article, Kenneth Arnold, was a pilot who'd reported flying saucers and UFOs before. Of the McDermitt lights, Arnold wrote,

> *About every ten years, in the desert near Oregon Canyon Ranch, which is located near McDermott [sic] Nevada, mysterious lights are seen at night by sheepherders and cowboys. Although rarely receiving publicity, these lights are a frequent subject of comment and conjecture on the part of the local ranchers.*

Could be some sort of mirage, car lights or . . . yes, the lights of hovering UFOs. Those who've witnessed the lights describe them as being pale lights with a reddish glow. A man who encountered the lights one night claimed that his horse was so frightened by the lights' sudden appearance that it bolted and was difficult to control.

McDermitt is a small town that straddles the Nevada-Oregon border. With fewer than 500 residents, it's safe to say there's not much going on around here. There's little to see and less to do, unless you count the mysterious lights. UFOs or some other phenomena? The mystery is yet to be solved.

Courtesy of Finetooth
via Wikimedia Commons

Alien Research Center

At first thought, this might sound like a place where you'll find a bunch of nerdy science types hovering around a computer screen as they try to decipher an SOS message from an extraterrestrial lost somewhere in the galaxy. No, this isn't that place. This is a fun place where the giant space alien beckons to you from beside the front door.

Inside you'll find treasures and everything an alien seeker might want or need: hats, mugs, T-shirts, and more. Do space aliens really look like this? I don't know. And what's more, I'm not all that anxious to encounter one and find out. If you are, this might be a good place to start your quest. But one thing, before you head down the road, whatever you do, don't forget to get that selfie of you and the giant space alien. It might come in handy one day—or night.

Courtesy of
Brian Pirwin, iStock

Atomic Museum Vegas

In the 1950s, during the early days of atomic bomb testing, savvy Las Vegas businesspeople saw an opportunity. With the action taking place about 65 miles away at the Nevada Proving Grounds, they offered their customers postcards to send home and sunglasses to wear as they watched mushroom clouds whirling up into the atmosphere. Creative bartenders filled up

Courtesy of Chon Kit Leong, Dreamstime.com

their tip jars by creating cocktails with atomic names. It was new, and it was exciting. And it would be many years before the dangers of all that testing were known.

If you're interested in learning more about the Nevada Test Site and the early days of US nuclear development, this museum should be on your list of places to see. Exhibits include earlier nuclear weapons like the B-54 backpack bomb, the Davy Crockett XM-388 projectile, and a real Phoebus-2A nuclear reactor. I thought it would be a lot bigger than that.

For those who like getting up close and personal, tours to the actual testing sites are offered on a limited basis. Strange as it seems, the ghost of a horribly scarred man is said to wander the museum, seeking something. What that might be, or who the ghost was, is anybody's guess.

Courtesy of
Bill Oberding

Chapter Four

That's Quirky, Nevada

There is odd and unusual and then there is Nevada-style quirky which runs the gamut from the flamboyant world renown pianist Liberace, a Las Vegas showroom favorite, to a pair of grave robbers who chose the tomb of historic state personages to rob, and on to the iconic Burning Man festival in the Black Rock Desert. It's all fun and it's all quirky.

The Skulls of Patrick and Susan Clayton

Lone Mountain Cemetery in Carson City is a picturesque old cemetery. In addition to Jennie Clemens, niece of Mark Twain, some of Nevada's earliest settlers, movers, and shakers rest here. Have your camera ready during your visit, as deer often congregate at the cemetery.

It was here in Lone Mountain Cemetery that a story of grave robbery takes place. File it under the most macabre category—it's an odd one. Early-day Nevada attorney, and founding member of the Democrat Party in Nevada, Patrick Henry Clayton had been resting in peace in the family mausoleum in the Lone Mountain Cemetery in Carson City since his death at age 51 in 1874. His beloved wife, Susan, joined him in his eternal rest in 1905.

All was well until Halloween night 1995 when a 38-year-old man and his girlfriend decided to do a little grave robbing. They wanted to buy drugs and had a cash buyer for the skulls.

The girlfriend got into the crypt and spent the night there, sawing the Claytons' skulls off at the shoulders. Everything went south (such plans always do) when the boyfriend was

Mark Twain Gets Angry

Every cemetery has stories to tell. Lone Mountain Cemetery is the final resting place of Jennie Clemens, beloved niece of Mark Twain (Samuel Clemens). After Jennie Clemens's death in 1864, Twain wrote a scathing article that appeared in the *Territorial Enterprise* about the exorbitant fees charged by undertakers, particularly those in Carson City. Twain was probably angry at the high cost of Jennie Clemens's funeral, which was $200 ($3,845 in today's dollars). Heartbroken at the loss of their only child, Orion and Mollie Clemens were suddenly faced with another crisis—the cost of her funeral. Two years later, they sold their home at a loss and left Nevada forever.

arrested in a Carson City motel with Mr. Clayton's skull in his backpack. Under a plea agreement, he would receive probation for testifying against his former girlfriend, who had Mrs. Clayton's skull and a buyer. So, he did.

Calling it one of the most bizarre, sickest, and weirdest cases he'd seen, Justice of the Peace John Tatro bound the former girlfriend over for trial. Five years after the incident on a snowy morning in late January 2000, a small ceremony was conducted at the Lone Mountain Cemetery, and the skulls were replaced in the mausoleum. And the Claytons can once again rest in peace. You're more than welcome to visit the cemetery and the interesting tomb of Mr. and Mrs. Clayton during daylight hours.

Black Rock City

There is nothing weird about a small city (say of nearly 70,000 people) that has its own post office, airport, restaurants, police force, and emergency crews. Nothing weird at all—unless that city is temporary and only exists for a week each year; this is what happens to Black Rock City. The city is erected on the playa in the Black Rock Desert to accommodate Burning Man attendees, known as Burners, who come from all over the world for the annual festival.

Burning Man began on a San Francisco beach in 1986 and was moved to the Black Rock Desert, where the event has grown to its current size with thousands of people participating. Burning Man is creativity, camaraderie,

spirituality, art cars, outlandish costumes, art for art's sake, music, public nudity, drugs, dust, and of course the wooden effigy of a man that is burned in a big bonfire at the end of the late summer event.

Burning Man Art for Everyone

Never mind all those dust-covered vehicles making their way through Reno and Northern Nevada traffic. They are Burners, and they are headed home. Their presence at the festival is a win for Nevada, which enjoys two distinct advantages of Burning Man. One is the boost to the local economy that happens when Burners come to town to do their shopping—they spend. The other is the art. Much of the art created for Burning Man eventually finds its way to Reno and Las Vegas so that even those who aren't able to attend the festival can enjoy it.

Courtesy of
Library of Congress

Wild Horses and Burros

Nevada boasts more wild horses and burros than any other state. With all the open spaces, it figures that thousands of wild horses and hundreds of wild burros are living in the Silver State. Those horses that live in the Virginia Range between Reno and Virginia are the most often spotted and photographed. And it's a fact of life that when you're driving south or north on Geiger Grade (State Route 341), you'd better be on the lookout for wild horses that sometimes wander onto the roadway and decide to stand there awhile. Granted, the horses are beautiful animals, and it's okay to grab a few photos, but keep your distance. Yes, even if they happen to be wandering the streets of Virginia City—which they often do—they are still wild animals.

To see the wild burros, you'll need to travel to the central part of the state, Mineral County to be exact. Here is where you'll find the old ghost town Marietta, located southwest of

Hawthorne. The first formally recognized wild burro range in the United States is about 68,000 acres, and that's plenty of room for the burros, which number just about a hundred, to roam.

Admire and photograph the burros all you want but keep your distance. Also, it's good to know that some of the land around this area is private, so heed the signs.

If you're traveling down Highway 395, you're liable to spot wild burros near the little town of Beatty as well.

Somewhere in Time, Maude

The 1980 film *Somewhere in Time* starring Christopher Reeve and Jane Seymour is a classic known to lovers of the romance movie genre the world over. And it all started in Virginia City with a photo at Piper's Opera House. Maude Adams, the woman in the photograph, had lived in Virginia City as a small child in 1874. While her father worked as a banker, Maude's mother appeared on stage under her maiden name in Virginia City. A few years later, the family moved to San Francisco. When Maude became a stage actress there, she also dropped the family name Kiskadden and used her mother's maiden name, Adams, so as not to embarrass her family. Thus, Maude Kiskadden became Maude Adams.

Moving forward a century, one summer day, science fiction writer Richard Matheson visited Virginia City during a family vacation and stopped at Piper's Opera House. There, he fell in

Virginia City's Crown Jewel

Piper's Opera House is one of only two historic opera houses still in use in Nevada. Built in 1885, Piper's Opera House is listed on the National Register of Historic Places. Many famous early 19th-century entertainers have appeared on the opera house's stage. Those from a more modern time include actors Errol Flynn and Hal Holbrook and singer Tennessee Ernie Ford. The opera house is available for rent and presents plays and other events throughout the year. It is also open during certain times of the year for tours.

As with most old theaters, Piper's is said to be haunted. But no one is quite certain just who the resident specter is.

Maude Adams

love, not with the old building, but with a portrait of a beautiful actress named Maude Adams. The writer, as writers are wont to do, let his creative imagination take free reign. What if time travel were possible? What if a present-day man were to fall in love with a long-ago actress? The photo of Maude Adams inspired Matheson to write a story.

Would he somehow be able to go back in time and be with her? He thought about it. In 1975, he wrote a romantic science-fiction novel, *Bid Time Return*, about just such a scenario. *Bid Time Return* was adapted into the 1980 film *Somewhere in Time.*

The Baskets of Dat So La Lee

Dat So La Lee (also known as Louisa Keyser) was a Native American woman of the Washoe of Northwestern Nevada, whose artistry in weaving baskets is unparalleled. She learned her craft as a young woman, and during her life she created over 300 baskets that were mostly woven of willow. Today, one of her baskets, if you are lucky enough to find one for sale, will command a very high price. Thankfully most of her works are in national museums so that we may all enjoy them. Dat So La Lee's baskets are on display at several museums, including the Smithsonian National Museum of the American Indian, the Metropolitan Museum of Modern Art in New York, and here in Nevada at the Nevada State Museum in Carson City and the Nevada Historical Society in Reno.

Dat So La Lee weaving a basket in 1900

Born sometime in 1829, with her birth name Dabuda, Dat So La Lee's career as a basket weaver began when she was hired by Amy and Abram Cohn in 1895 as their laundress. When they realized she was a gifted basket weaver, the Cohns hired her to create baskets for their emporium in Carson City. In return for her baskets, Dat So La Lee received a house, food, and health care. The basket-selling venture proved a success for the Cohns and Dat So La Lee.

Art in a Basket

Carson City shopkeeper Abram Cohn is credited with discovering Dat So La Lee's artistry when she worked for his family as a housekeeper. Acting as her promoter, Cohn took Dat So La Lee to the 1893 Great Chicago exposition where her baskets were well received. While his wife, Amy, lectured and wrote about Dat So La Lee and her baskets, Abram Cohn sold them at his shop. Abram Cohn built Dat So La Lee a small home located at 331 West Proctor Street. The home, also known as the Louisa Keyser home, was placed on the National Register of Historic Places in 1994. The home is a private residence, so be mindful of this when driving or walking past.

Dat So La Lee died on December 6, 1925, and is buried in the Stewart Cemetery in Carson City. A historic marker at her gravesite reads, Myriads of stars shine over the graves of our ancestors. Some believe this may have been the name of one of her baskets.

Double Negative and City

Earth art (also known as land art) is an art form created in nature using natural materials such as soil and rock. Nevada's foremost land artist, landscaper Michael Heizer has been creating his earth art since the 1960s. Tremendous amounts of rock and soil are often moved in the making of this type of art; from 1969 to 1970, 240,000 tons of rock were displaced in the production of his *Double Negative* located at the eastern edge of Mormon Mesa near Overton. *Double Negative* is two enormous 50-feet-deep and 30-feet-wide trenches that were cut and together span 1,500 feet. And it is the largest sculpture in the world.

At more than a mile and a half long and a half mile wide, *City* is humongous . . . Michael Heizer's latest work in the middle of the Nevada desert was 50 years in the making and is now open to the public on a very limited reservation basis; only six tickets are sold per day.

One Man's Art

Michael Heizer is a pioneer in land art, an American movement that came into being in the 1960s and '70s. Heizer's *City* is the largest contemporary art ever completed and was created at a cost of $40 million. Some may think that land art is transitory. That isn't always true. And there is no reason to believe that *City* won't be there in Lincoln County for a very long time to come. In 2015, President Obama created by proclamation the Basin and Range National Monument, which is about 704,000 acres, and *City* is within those acres.

Very few people even know *City*'s exact location, beyond the fact that it is somewhere in Lincoln County. For now, the curious must be content with visiting Heizer's earlier work, *Double Negative*, which is currently owned by the Museum of Contemporary Art (Los Angeles). If you want to see what land art in Nevada is all about, in regards to *Double Negative* or *City*, plan on a trip, but remember that it is only accessible by four-wheel drive.

Courtesy of Thure Johnson, Wikimedia Commons

Joshua Trees

You won't see them just anywhere. And they aren't trees at all. Those unique and unusual plants that dot the desert highway are actually the genus Yucca and the species *Yucca Brevifolia* (Yucca palms). They can reach a height of 40 feet, and they stand along the roadways of certain areas of Central and Southern Nevada. Native to the arid Mojave Desert region, Joshua trees are long-lived with a lifespan of 500 years.

Quick, take a picture! You won't find them anywhere else but the Mojave Desert region of California, Nevada, Utah, and Arizona, and then only at elevations from 2,000 to 6,000 feet.

No one is certain when these rare Yucca palms were first dubbed Joshua trees. A widely accepted tale is that Mormon settlers to this area of Nevada were the first to call them Joshua trees. And that may be true. Regardless of how, or why, the name has stuck, and people who live in this region know them as nothing but Joshua trees.

Courtesy of Frank Debonis, iStock

Rustlin' Shoes

An old saying holds that if you build a better mousetrap, the world will beat a path to your door. "Crazy" Tex Hazelwood took those words to heart. Only he wasn't trying to get the world to beat a path to his door so much as he was intent on creating a foolproof way to rustle a few head of cattle.

This was during the 1920s, and a ranch near Elko kept coming up short on cattle. A cattle thief was about, but how could they stop him when they found only the hoofprints of other cattle around the enclosure? There were no footprints, tire prints, or any other evidence that a thief even existed. After giving the matter a lot of thought, the sheriff came up with the idea of watching the cattle day and night. Surely the thief would eventually show himself. And one night, he did. And on his feet were  the most unusual shoes anyone had ever seen. It seems "Crazy" Tex Hazelwood was a fashion designer of sorts. He'd designed and created a unique pair of shoes that resembled skates with cow hoofs as heels. No wonder they'd had such a hard time catching him.

His excuse was he didn't think the ranch would miss a few head of cattle. But they had. And it was off to jail for Tex Hazelwood. If you've got to see them, Tex's rustlin' shoes are on display at the Northeastern Nevada Museum in Elko.

Liberace Lived on Shirley Avenue

Courtesy of Bill Oberding

Who was the first entertainer to wear flamboyant costumes while performing on stage in Las Vegas? No, it wasn't Elvis, Prince, or Elton John. It was Liberace. And he was also the first Las Vegas performer to command and receive a hefty salary. The classically trained pianist charmed audiences with his saucy banter while playing contemporary tunes on a grand piano bedecked with candelabras.

But it was his over-the-top sequined, bejeweled, and fur-trimmed costumes that really captured his audience's imagination. During his show, he gave the audience a chance to really ogle the sequins as he strutted out into the audience, assuring them that he was laughing all the way to the bank. And with a salary of thousands of dollars a week, why shouldn't he?

For his home, Liberace bought two houses in a middle-class neighborhood and had them converted into one house. From the outside, the house was just your ordinary, run-of-the-mill house, but inside was a different story altogether.

The house was filled with treasures. The walls were covered with mirrors; a large fountain in the foyer welcomed guests, and on the ceiling were paintings of Liberace himself. In the bathroom was a bathtub big enough for three or four with gold-toned faucets. The master bedroom featured a ceiling of cherubs done by an Italian master painter in the style of the Sistine Chapel. And, of course, the backyard featured a swimming pool in the shape of a piano.

Ghost, the Dog

Every dog (and cat) deserves a loving forever home. Miraculously, and against all odds, it looks as if Ghost has gotten the chance to find his forever home. Had he been dumped in the desert as a puppy, or had he wandered away from home? Either way, his chances of survival in the desert's hostile environment were not good. When he was spotted wandering a Henderson neighborhood with a pack of coyotes, people wondered what had caused this handsome white dog to join a pack of coyotes. The dog has strong survival instincts.

Courtesy hpzima, iStock

They call the white dog Ghost; no one is sure what his real name might have been, or if he ever even had any other name. For the past several months before he was rescued, he was living with coyotes in the desert just outside of Henderson's city limits.

Every gambler knows that luck can change at the drop of a card. Ghost may not be a gambler, but his luck has changed. He has been rescued and is receiving medical attention for the numerous injuries he suffered while living in the wild with coyotes. A GoFundMe page was set up to help with those costly vet bills, and the loving and happy dog known as Ghost was once again thriving in the home of his rescuer.

But it seems a custody battle may be brewing over Ghost. A family came forward with photos and proof that Ghost was really a dog named Hades and he belonged to them. Ghost, aka Hades, was given to the family with the photos. There is no such thing as too much love, and luckily for this dog, he has plenty of people who love and want to care for him.

Ethel M. Chocolate Factory and Botanical Cactus Garden

Helen Keller is quoted as having said, "Life is short and unpredictable. Eat the dessert first!" I concur. And I'll add this is especially true if it involves chocolate. This is where Ethel M. Chocolate Factory in Henderson comes in. Take my word; this is one of Las Vegas's sweetest experiences. And it's free and open to the public. How sweet is that?

On the tour, you'll see how they make some of that luscious candy and look in the kitchen where they make peanut brittle. Satin crèmes and caramels, it all makes my mouth water just to write these words. Made in small batches with no preservatives, lucky there's the gift shop to grab some goodies.

But there's more here. Enjoy your chocolate and step out of the factory and into the botanical cactus garden, which happens to be the largest in the state of Nevada. There are three acres and 300 species of drought-tolerant desert-dwelling plants. The cactus garden, like the chocolate factory, is free and open all year round.

Courtesy ionna_alexa, iStock

Bing Crosby's Denim Tuxedo

In the 1940s and '50s, Bing Crosby was a household name. He was a big celebrity. BIG, with all the road movies with Bob Hope and hits like "I'm Dreaming of a White Christmas." He was a superstar. He could have lived anywhere he wanted. But Bing liked Nevada, particularly the Elko area, where he owned several ranches.

Down to earth and friendly, Crosby was well-liked by his neighbors and fellow ranchers. In 1948, Bing was appointed Elko's honorary mayor, thus making him the first person to ever

Bing Crosby's denim tuxedo on display

Levi Tuxedos

be honorary mayor of a Nevada city. Honorary mayor or not, Bing hit a snag in Vancouver, British Columbia, three years later when a swank hotel refused him and his friends service because they were dressed inappropriately in—denim. The story's been told and retold dozens of times; in the Reno version, Bing was at the Riverside Hotel in downtown Reno when a snooty maître d' refused to sit him at a table.

Regardless of who did the refusal, imagine how foolish the swanks felt once they realized they'd just denied rooms to one of the world's superstars and his pals. A lot of bowing and scraping, apologies all around, and an exception was made for the denim-clad bunch. The good-natured Crosby laughed it off. And when he returned to Elko, he told friends about the Bing Crosby blunder.

Someone came up with a great idea; what if Bing had a denim tuxedo?

And so, they commissioned the Levi Strauss Company to design and make a special tuxedo for Crosby. A matching tuxedo was also created for Elko's elected mayor, Dave Dotta. Crosby loved the tuxedo and wore it at all formal occasions in Elko, including the premiere of his 1951 movie *Here Comes the Groom*.

In 2014, the Levi Strauss Company recreated 200 limited-edition Bing Crosby denim tuxedos, which were almost identical to the original. A recent listing on eBay offered one for $2,300.

Goldwell Open Air Museum at Rhyolite

The Goldwell Museum and Rhyolite ghost town are located in the Bullfrog Hills, about 120 miles from Las Vegas. But who could imagine a museum in the middle of the Mojave Desert? The Danish artist Albert Szukalski could. In 1984, Szukalski started things by creating the ghostly art sculpture *The Last Supper* at a location outside of Rhyolite. The sculpture depicts Leonardo da Vinci's painting *The Last Supper*. It's one of the most photographed sculptures at the park. It is by no means the only piece of art on display.

Be Careful Where You Step

Quick—if you're certain it wasn't a rattlesnake, ask yourself if it was the wind you just heard, or was it a ghost? Rhyolite is a ghost town, after all. So, it's no wonder that ghosts are rumored to lurk here among the sagebrush and the old buildings. Ghost enthusiasts believe there's a spooky side to Rhyolite, and ghosts exist out here in the Nevada desert as surely as rattlesnakes and other desert-hardy creatures.

The larger-than-life-size mosaic sofa is probably one of the museum's most popular pieces with those looking for a good selfie spot. The museum is located on the eastern edge of Death Valley, so expect warmer-than-elsewhere temperatures. Wear comfortable shoes; you'll be doing some walking as you explore other interesting art pieces throughout this outdoor setting. Camera buffs take note: the views looking across the desert here are spectacular.

After exploring the museum, you surely will want to see Rhyolite, an old ghost town of crumbling buildings and lots of history. The train station is still standing. But the train doesn't run here anymore. During its 1906 heyday, Rhyolite was served by the trains that came and went from Las Vegas and Tonopah. It's hard to imagine in the stillness of the desert, but 5,000 people once lived here in Rhyolite. By 1914, it was all over for the mines, Rhyolite, and the trains.

The art and the old ghost town are enough to keep you busy for hours. One word of caution: This is the desert, so be aware and step lightly. There are rattlesnakes here in the desert.

Before you leave Rhyolite, consider that it offers some of the clearest skies in the United States. Photographers regularly come here to take photos of the night sky.

Clown Motel

Coulrophobia is a real thing; it's the fear of clowns, and if you happen to suffer from this fear, it's best to pass this story by. Tonopah's famous, or not so, Clown Motel is all about clowns.

All those stuffed clowns and clown photos. Everywhere you look, there's a clown—thousands of them; the motel is a unique place to spend a night and boast about it the next day. And if you happen to be a fan of clowns, well there simply is no better place to spend the night. Some of the rooms even have clowns painted on the walls. But fair warning, there is one particular clown who looks decidedly wicked. Having slept in this room a couple of times, I will say that he gave me pause as I drifted off to sleep. There are those who will tell you that the place is haunted. And that could well be. Seems like the perfect place for a ghostly clown of circuses past to hang out.

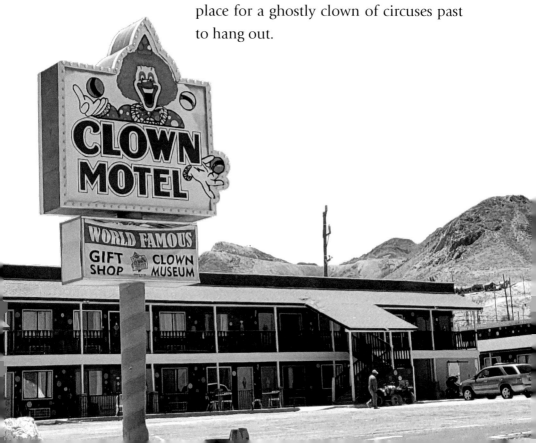

A Great Little Town

Tonopah's not that big and certainly not that busy. Aside from the Mizpah Hotel, there are some great little restaurants in town. Check out the Tonopah Historic Mining Park and the Central Nevada Museum and take a look around. Or better yet, wait until after dark and then look straight up at the night sky; this is one of the best places in the United States to stargaze. There is none of the light pollution common to larger cities like Las Vegas, 240 miles to the south, and Reno about the same distance to the north.

But let's not forget that the Clown Motel sits in full view of the old Tonopah Cemetery. Walk right out the front door, and there's the cemetery. Which is worse, clowns or ghosts? I'll leave that up to you to decide.

Ward Charcoal Ovens State Historic Park

Getting here takes some doing. And be warned, it's not the place to bring your brand-new sports car. The road is bumpy and not paved. But Ward Charcoal Ovens State Historic Park is well worth the effort. The park is located about 20 miles from Ely. Once you get here, be prepared to be amazed. The six beehive-shaped charcoal ovens are 30 feet high by 27 feet in diameter and are truly man-made wonders.

The ovens were built and used from 1876 to 1879. And those who aren't familiar with early-day silver processing techniques may wonder what the ovens were used for.

Italian immigrants (Carbonari) built the ovens near the town of Ward, to create charcoal that was necessary for processing silver ore. But the amount of silver here in Ward was never what it was in other parts of Nevada. And just like so many other Nevada mining towns, Ward's population dwindled from nearly 2,000 to 200 or so once the silver was depleted.

The ovens were no longer needed. But they didn't stand idle. It's said that the well-made ovens served as shelters for travelers and even hideouts for robbers. In 1971, the Ward Charcoal Ovens were listed on the National Register of Historic Places.

Privately owned until 1956, the Ward Charcoal Ovens State Historic Park was designated as a state park in 1994. If you visit, bring a picnic lunch and plan on spending the day—and maybe a night. There's no need to hurry.

The park offers facilities for camping and picnicking. And whatever you do, don't forget to take some selfies.

Courtesy Famartin,
Wikimedia Commons

The Man Who Was Hanged Three Times

Nevada was four years old on October 30, 1868, when 21-year-old Rufus Anderson was led to the gallows in Austin. He'd shot Noble T. Slocum in cold blood and was condemned to death. As a bone-chilling, winter-like wind blew across the scaffold, Anderson faced the crowd and calmly asked for forgiveness. His arms were tied behind him and a black hood placed over his head.

"I commend my soul to thee," he whispered as the noose was slipped around his neck.

And then something went wrong. The trap was sprung and Rufus Anderson, rather than being hoisted into the next world, dropped to the ground with a thud. Did I mention that Anderson was a large and heavy man? The crowd fell silent. Someone gasped; another screamed in horror as he was carried back to the scaffold and the noose again slipped around his neck. This time,

Austin, Nevada, in 1868

A Little Town of Churches

Lest you think Austin was named after that other city in Texas, it wasn't. It was named after Alvah Austin, business partner of David Buell, who mapped out the town in 1862. Like countless other Nevada mining towns, Austin saw its population dwindle as rich silver mining gave out. Today it's a tiny historic town on Nevada's Loneliest Highway and is noted for its three historic churches built between 1866 and 1878, its old cemetery, and the former Lander County Courthouse where the lynching of Richard Jennings took place in 1881. The old courthouse was placed on the Register of Historic Places in 2003 and is used as county offices.

he would surely swing. But he didn't. The same thing happened when the trap was sprung once again. Two failed attempts enraged the crowd. "This is butchery!" men roared.

If not for the armed guards who stood nearby, the unruly crowd might have overtaken the scaffold and set Rufus Anderson free. Some of the men angrily demanded Anderson's life be spared after such a debacle. But a death warrant is a death warrant. After some deliberation, it was decided that the unconscious Anderson was just too hefty for the hanging to work properly. But justice must be met. And so, Anderson was strapped to a chair; he would be hanged in a seated position. Before the deed was done, he awoke and asked for water.

With that request filled, the noose was placed once more around his neck and the trap dropped. The third time was a charm; the third and final hanging of Rufus B. Anderson was successful.

Rocky Mountain Oyster Fry

This annual Virginia City event takes place on the Saturday before St. Patrick's Day and is the biggest St. Patrick's Day celebration in Nevada. It brings crowds of fun lovers up Geiger Grade. The wearin' of the green, the live music, the merchants and vendors, the saloons—the fun factor is a ten on a scale of one to five. And you've worked up an appetite and are ready to eat!

There are so many different ways to cook a Rocky Mountain oyster; who's to say which way is the best? Yessir, you're hungry right up to the time you come to know just that a Rocky Mountain oyster comes from a different part of the steer than a T-bone steak does—they don't call this the "testicle festival" for nothing. If you're one of the brave and adventuresome gourmands, you'll smile and take a bite and munch with the best of them. If not, you'll say no thanks, choose sides like slaw and corn on the cob, down a green beer, and call it good.

Just to Think, Mining Started It All

In the spring and summer, there is always something going on, and something to see and do in Virginia City. After you've tasted this unusual delicacy, you might want to guzzle some green drinks and then take some time to stop at the visitors center and get a list of just what there is here in this historic old, mining town.

After eating, or before, you might want to join the Ballbreaker Saloon Crawl, which visits many of Virginia City's amazing old saloons. It's enough to turn the streets green. Look again, there's a green line going down the center of C Street. St. Paddy would be so proud!

Oyster Fry Parade. Courtesy of Virginia City Tourism

Berlin-Ichthyosaur State Park

The Berlin mining company was established in 1896 and soon Berlin was a thriving gold and silver mining camp with more than 200 people living and working there. Berlin was different from other Nevada mining towns. Its miners often encountered strange-looking fossils and bones as they worked. The more resourceful decorated their cabins with the larger fossils and used the round vertebrae as dinner plates.

These miners had no idea that they were using the fossils of creatures that had lived millions of years earlier. Nor did they know that they were the mysterious marine reptile, ichthyosaur, and they swam in the ancient Lahontan Sea that had once covered most of Nevada. They were giants that attained a length of more than 50 feet. And their fossils set Nevada apart as the

Courtesy Wirestock, iStock.com

only state in the United States with a complete skeleton of the extinct reptile. No wonder Nevada claims the ichthyosaur as its state fossil.

Berlin didn't last; by 1911, its mines in the nearby tunnels that had produced nearly a million dollars were played out. As people packed up and moved on, Berlin slowly sank into decline. In 1928, the fossilized remains of the ichthyosaurs were discovered by a member of the scientific community. Decades later, paleontologists with the University of California Berkeley came to Berlin to begin excavating the area in 1954.

In 1957, the Berlin-Ichthyosaur State Park was established in order to protect and display what would ultimately become North America's largest concentration of Ichthyosaur fossils; excavation of the site would continue well into the 1960s. During this time, at least 40 ichthyosaurs were unearthed at Berlin. These were named *Shonisaurus Popularis* because the site of their discovery is near the Shoshone Mountain Range.

The 1,153-acre Berlin-Ichthyosaur State Park is a registered natural landmark and the ghost town of Berlin is on the National Register of Historic Places.

Three Unique Courthouses

There are 17 counties in Nevada. And every one of those counties is rightfully proud of their courthouse. But three county courthouses in use today are unique enough to warrant a look: Pershing, Storey, and Esmerelda Counties are the three included here.

The small city of Lovelock has bragging rights to something that not even Hollywood, Chicago, or New York has. It's the historic Pershing County courthouse and it is believed to be the only round courthouse still in use in the United States. The courthouse was designed by Nevada's preeminent, early 20th-century architect Frederic DeLongchamps, who also designed courthouses for Washoe, Clark, Lyon, and Douglas Counties.

Completed in June 1921, the Pershing County Courthouse was placed on the National Register of Historic Places in 1983.

The Storey County Courthouse in Virginia City has an often-seen Lady Justice standing atop its main entrance. There is nothing unusual in this, except that this Lady Justice is unblindfolded and that is unusual as far as courthouses go. Built in 1875, the Storey County Courthouse is the oldest continuously operated courthouse in Nevada.

Esmerelda County has fewer than 200 residents, but its courthouse built in

1907 is still in use today. That's unusual in the Silver State. As their populations dwindled, many towns saw their county seat status awarded to larger, more populace cities. This left several old courthouses being abandoned as far as legal matters go.

A.D. 1907
COURT HOUSE

Fremont Street Experience

Mobster Benjamin Bugsy Siegel is credited with being the first to envision just how powerful of an entertainment venue Las Vegas could be. He saw the city's potential, but in his wildest dreams Bugsy could never have imagined how Fremont Street of his time would be transformed into what it is today. This five-block-long section of Fremont Street is located in what is known as the historic district, and it's an entertainment venue of sights and sounds, shops, restaurants, live entertainment, music, and more.

Look up at the light shows on the giant canopy. And there's Slotzilla's zip line, which zips riders over the Fremont Experience, a fast-moving bird's-eye view if you will. The only

question is—do you want to fly superhero style on superhero-zoom or would you prefer to be seated on the zip-zilla zip line?

The Fremont Street Experience is free to walk through. But it might not be the place to bring young children. There are street vendors and live entertainers and so many shops that there is so much temptation; no one should expect to walk out of here without spending a few dollars. Don't worry about time constraints; the Fremont Experience never closes. Bugsy would no doubt be very proud of his old stomping grounds.

Bliss Dance

In 1958, there were two sci-fi films that dealt with two people who'd grown to gigantic proportions because of menacing space aliens and top-secret science experiments in the Nevada desert: *The Colossal Man* and *Attack of the 50 Foot Woman*. In their anger and frustration, the giant man and woman run amok. He rampages through Las Vegas.

Fast-forward to the present time at the Park on the Strip; here you'll find the 40-foot-tall *Bliss Dance* sculpture. Originally created for display on the playa during Burning Man 2010, *Bliss Dance*, like all unique and wonderful things, has found its way to Las Vegas. The first in a series of three, *Bliss Dance* was created by artist Marco Cochrane, whose collaborator and model for the project was singer/dancer Deja Solis. In a delightful way, *Bliss Dance* reminds us that it's a new day. Women are no longer constrained by the standards of a long-ago era.

Courtesy of Kobby Dagan

Bliss Dance is located at the Park, a place the whole family can enjoy. You might want to catch a basketball game, a boxing match, or a concert at T-Mobile Arena. Before or after, keep in mind that there are some fun restaurants, including the Hello Kitty Café. Who wouldn't love a Hello Kitty cookie, croissant, or donut? Better yet, there is a slew of Hello Kitty merchandise sure to thrill any Hello Kitty aficionada's heart. Then there's the Shake Shack—yum, that tiramisu shake sounds heavenly. Ride the Big Apple Coaster, and then do some shopping at the nearby New York New York.

It's a spectacular sight to behold, day or night. But it is at night when it is lit up that *Bliss Dance* enchants. Mark this as another of those sites you just can't miss when next you visit Las Vegas.

Thunderbird Lodge

Although not nearly as large and grand, Thunderbird Lodge is Nevada's answer to California's Winchester Mystery House in San Jose. The man who conceived Thunderbird Lodge, George Whittell, was born to a life of privilege and wealth with his every whim indulged. When his father died in 1922, the 40-year-old George Whittell Jr. was left with an estate of about $30 million. While the rest of the country struggled with the Depression, eccentric George Whittell, who preferred to be called Captain, inherited more money than he could ever spend in his lifetime.

Fourteen years later, Whittell tired of city life and began planning a summer home on the shores of Lake Tahoe. After all, he owned 40,000 acres and 27 miles of the eastern shore of Lake Tahoe. As architect of his Thunderbird Lodge, he chose Frederic DeLongchamps, who'd designed several courthouses and homes in Northern Nevada, and was one of Nevada's top architects of the time. A man ahead of his time in this regard,

An Inadvertent Gift

By all accounts, George Whittell was not a humanitarian. He didn't develop or subdivide his 40,000 acres so that he wouldn't have anybody living near him. He disdained neighbors. In doing so, he kept the land pristine and beautiful so that future generations might enjoy it. This was purely unintentional on his part. You will see just what a gift Whittell gave to people when you visit the south shore of Lake Tahoe (and you absolutely should). Note all the high-rise hotel casinos that cover the land.

George Whittell wanted his home and all buildings, including the boathouse, on the property to blend with their surroundings. None were to detract from the beauty of Lake Tahoe itself.

DeLongchamps used master craftsmen, ironworkers, and stonemasons who'd learned their trade at the Steward Indian School in Carson City to bring the idea to fruition. Rumor has it that George Whittell carried on scandalous affairs behind the rock walls of Thunderbird Lodge and even kept a pet lion and an elephant on the premises.

If you'd like to see how the fabulously wealthy lived at Lake Tahoe in the mid-20th century, you're in luck. Tours of Thunderbird Lodge are offered from mid-spring to early fall.

Hoover Dam

Work on the dam began in 1930 and it was completed in 1935. The work was grueling and dangerous, and some men lost their lives while building the dam. That said, I'll do a bit of myth busting here by letting you know that those men who died while working on the dam were not buried in concrete where they fell so that work could continue on schedule. It sounds horrific, but it's a story that's been told forever about Hoover Dam.

Hoover Dam (originally called Boulder Dam) was created to harness the power of the Colorado River, to produce hydroelectric power, and to prevent flooding in Southern Arizona, Nevada, and California. The dam project on the border of Nevada and Arizona provided jobs for thousands of men who had seen

Courtesy of trekandshoot, iStock

Art Is Where You Find It

A visit to the dam should also include a visit to Boulder City and the Boulder City Hoover Dam Museum, where you'll learn about Hoover Dam and the people who built it. The museum is housed in the historic Boulder Dam Hotel; a slew of rich and famous people, including Shirley Temple, Bette Davis, and Howard Hughes, once spent some time here. According to some, at least one ghostly person is still in residence at the hotel. While you're here, take time to look at the *Alabam* statue on the corner of Nevada Way and Ash Street. *Alabam* by artist Steven Liguori honors the men who kept the dam workers' outhouses clean and supplied with toilet paper. Do I have to tell you what a great selfie opportunity this is?

employment vanish during the Great Depression. These men settled their families in nearby Boulder City (a town created for dam workers and their families) and Las Vegas. Boulder City, because it was a federal company town, had very strict no gambling and no alcohol rules. Although it is no longer a company town, Boulder City is one of only two cities in Nevada that does not allow gambling.

Each year, over seven million people visit and tour the Hoover Dam, which is about 35 miles north of Las Vegas.

Ely's Murals

If Paris is the city of lights, then Ely is the city of Murals. First things first; this is Ely, a tiny town of about 4,000 residents located approximately 200 miles north of Las Vegas. The name Ely rhymes with "mealy" and not "sigh." Now that that's been cleared up, let's take a look at some of what this little town offers visitors. Railroad buffs know of course that the Northern Nevada Railway Museum is located here in Ely. Think the Polar Express, the Haunted Ghost Train, and 90-minute passenger train rides and some informative history events. And then there is the art.

These are the more than 20 colorful murals depicting early Ely's history that cover many of Ely's buildings. There are self-guided walking tours so that you won't miss a single mural. You can pick up a free brochure map at just about any downtown Ely business and explore the city of murals.

The Architecture of Paul Revere Williams

The distinguished African American architect Paul Revere Williams was not a Nevadan; nonetheless, he left his mark on Nevada by creating some of the state's most iconic buildings. In 1939, Williams was commissioned to design the First Church of Christ, Scientist on Riverside Drive across from the Truckee River on the edge of downtown Reno.

The resulting building was neoclassical in style and still stands to this day. Williams also designed homes and apartment buildings in Reno. In Las Vegas, he designed the modernistic La Concha Motel lobby. Although the motel was torn down,

La Concha Motel, courtesy of Library of Congress

And So the Design Lives On

Nearly 60 years after Williams designed it, the First Church of Christ, Scientist building on Riverside Drive In downtown Reno was purchased in 1998 with matching funds of Reno philanthropist Moya Lear and the Reno community. The building was renamed the Lear Theater and repurposed for use as a local theater and arts event center. The Lear Theater is a place of cultural importance to the city of Reno, which took over ownership of the building in 2021. The goal is to rehabilitate the property so that it may be used as a community theater.

the lobby building is used as the visitors center at the Neon Museum in Las Vegas. Another of his designs can be seen at the Guardian Angel Cathedral, which serves more than 73,000 Catholics and is visited by thousands of tourists every year.

Williams also designed homes for some of Hollywood's most famous stars. In 1957, Williams became the first African American to be voted a fellow of the American Institute of Architects.

Early Days on the Silver Screen

With its varied locations, Nevada is a favorite of filmmakers. One of the earliest films shot in the state was probably *The Tonopah Stampede for Gold*. The 1913 four-reeler featured

Rex Bell and Clara Bow

Nevada Governor Tasker Oddie and Tonopah silver discoverer Jim Butler, who appeared as themselves in the movie. The film told the story of an early-day gold rush to Tonopah and may not even have ever been released.

In 1926, the Samuel Goldwyn Company came to the Black Rock Desert to film scenes for the silent movie *The Winning of Barbara Worth* starring Ronald Coleman, Vilma Banky, and Gary Cooper.

Today, Las Vegas has eclipsed Hollywood as the entertainment capital of the world. And nearly every star has a home in Las Vegas. Silent-screen star Clara Bow, known as the It Girl, was one of the first film stars to live in Southern Nevada. When she married cowboy actor Rex Bell in 1931, they bought the Walking Box Ranch as a working 400,000-acre ranch, and Clara Bow retired from acting to live on the ranch near Las Vegas.

Rex Bell delved into politics and was elected Nevada Lieutenant Governor in 1954. He was lieutenant governor when he appeared in his last film, *The Misfits* (which was filmed in

Filmmaking has changed much since those early days. Hundreds of movies and TV shows have been shot in the Silver State since the silent *The Tonopah Stampede for Gold* was filmed here in 1913. Naturally, some Nevada locations are more popular with filmmakers than others. But which Nevada location has appeared in film more than any other? Those who are curious about this may be surprised to learn that it isn't Lake Tahoe or the iconic Las Vegas Strip, although these two locations are very popular with filmmakers. Drum roll, please—the Nevada location that appears in film more often than any other is—Hoover Dam.

Reno and other Northern Nevada locations), starring Marilyn Monroe and Clark Gable in 1960. Incidentally, the film was also Monroe's and Gable's last film.

On the morning of January 15, 1942, actress Carole Lombard (wife of Clark Gable) was traveling back to Hollywood from Indiana when her plane crashed on Mt. Potosi, approximately 30 miles southwest of Las Vegas. While sitting on the front porch of her ranch house, Clara Bow was said to have witnessed the fireball on Mt. Potosi and didn't learn until later what had happened and that Lombard was on board.

Blue Jeans

Just about everyone you know probably has a pair of jeans. They're the go-to article of clothing that goes with anything— they can be dressed up with sequins or down with a flannel shirt. And if it weren't for a Reno tailor by the name of Jacob Youphes, we'd be making very different fashion statements.

Jacob Davis

Youphes immigrated to the United States from Latvia in 1854. Wanting to be more accepted, he changed his last name to Davis. In New York, Davis did what he knew best, tailoring. But he'd heard of the opportunities that waited in the west and didn't stay long. Davis headed first to Virginia City and then to Reno, where he opened his tailoring shop on North Virginia Street downtown.

In 1873, Davis's life, and indeed the fashion industry itself, were changed forever when the wife of a hefty husband happened into the shop one day. She had a problem; her husband kept ripping out the seams and pockets of his work pants and she was tired of constantly repairing them. Did Mr. Davis have a solution to make hubby's trousers more durable? Indeed, he did. Jacob Davis created a pair of work pants out of sturdy canvas, and just for good measure he reinforced the seams and pockets with copper rivets. The wife was thrilled. The husband was happy; his pants weren't in constant need of repair. And Jacob Davis's idea caught on.

We All Wear Jeans

May 20, 1873, is considered to be the birthday of blue jeans—it is the date the Levi Strauss Company received the patent for blue jeans, which were originally called waist overalls. No one could have seen how jeans would define fashion, changing the day-to-day attire of people around the world. Today, jeans are ubiquitous in women's wardrobes. But they wouldn't be released for women until 1934, and it would be another decade before they became popular wear for women. President Jimmy Carter and first lady Roslyn were the first occupants of the White House to wear jeans at 1600 Pennsylvania Avenue.

When he heard of the pants, Levi Strauss signed a contract with Davis to head up his San Francisco factory. And the rest is fashion history. The city of Reno proudly placed a plaque downtown on North Virginia Street to commemorate the invention that changed the way we dress forever.

Jacob Davis's Tailor Shop marker on Virginia Street

In Cold Blood's Connection to Nevada

In 1966, Truman Capote's book *In Cold Blood* was published. The book was a huge success and is the second bestselling true crime book in history. The book and the subsequent film brought renewed attention to the cold-blooded killing of the Clutter family in Holcomb, Kansas. *In Cold Blood* chronicles the 1959 murders; fresh out of prison, two losers, Richard Hickock and Perry Smith, drove to the Clutter family's home on November 15, 1959, and slaughtered the entire family for a safe full of money that didn't exist.

After the murders, Hickock and Smith hit the road, robbing and stealing their way across the county. They ended up in Nevada, where Perry Smith was born 30 years earlier. Smith had recently lived in Las Vegas and wanted to return to retrieve

Las Vegas Reads

If you're at the Mob Museum near the spot where Smith and Hickock were arrested, Truman Capote might be on your mind. And so might literature. Good, you're only about five minutes away from the Writer's Block, an independently owned bookshop, coffee shop, and young writers workshop. And there are book clubs. Among them are the Reading Women Book Club, the Shakespeare Reading Book Club, and the Bourbon Book Club. The clubs meet once a month at the Writer's Block to discuss their favorites. And of course, there is a selection of new books. A great place for readers and writers, and I think Truman Capote would have approved.

some personal items. Their stay in Las Vegas would not be a long one. They were arrested on December 30, 1959; incidentally, that arrest took place a few blocks from the post office/federal courthouse building that is today the Mob Museum. Hickock willingly admitted his guilt and signed a statement saying that he and Smith had murdered the Clutter family.

On January 6, 1960, six days after their arrest, Smith and Hickock met with officers of the Kansas Bureau of Investigation who escorted them back to Kansas to stand trial for their crimes. After having been convicted, Hickock and Smith were hanged for the murders on April 16, 1965.

Courtesy of Library of Congress

Genoa's Candy Dance

This is Nevada. And we have our own way of pronouncing things. The quaint little town of Genoa is one of those things. Genoa in Nevada sounds nothing like that city in Italy. In Nevada, Genoa rhymes with "Balboa." So now that you know that, let's talk about Genoa's annual Candy Dance, the September event that brings thousands of visitors.

In 1919, Genoa wanted streetlights. But there was no money in the town's coffers. Lillian Virgin Finnegan had an idea. A dance would bring people out. And as an added incentive, candy could be passed out to those attending. The event was a big success and Genoa could purchase its streetlights. The event's popularity increased and became hereafter known as the Candy Dance.

Two Towns, One History

With its Mormon Station State Historic Park, antique stores, oldest bar in Nevada, and its restaurants, Genoa is worth a visit any time of the year. Just be aware that deer wander the town's streets at will. Genoa holds a special place in Nevada's history. It was here that the first seat of government began before Nevada achieved statehood and while it was still part of the Nevada Territory. Genoa was founded by Mormon settlers in 1851 and claims to be the oldest town in Nevada—but then again, nearby Dayton makes the same claim. And placer miners were founding the area around Gold Canyon about the same time as the Mormon traders came to Genoa. But let's not quibble. Let's just say that both towns are uniquely woven into Nevada's history and leave it at that.

Today, the Candy Dance is a two-day event with music, arts and crafts, and food, and yes, candy. Artists and craftspeople come from all over to show and sell their stuff. It has grown into such a popular event that attendees must park elsewhere and be shuttled into Genoa, since there just aren't enough parking spaces.

Genoa Community Church

Wild horses near the Savage Mansion in Virginia City

Chapter Five

Nevada Things to See and Do

What does Nevada have that no other state has? For starters there is the memorial to gangster Bugsy Siegel, the old Nevada State Prison which presents tours and ghost hunts, a rib cook off and the Mob Museum. And proving that Nevadans love their food there are lots of festivals like Fallon's cantaloupe festival and Sparks' Best in the West rib cook off—tasty!

• •

"Welcome to Fabulous Las Vegas" Sign

Nevada's largest city, Las Vegas is synonymous with a round-the-clock lifestyle, high-rise hotel casino resorts, glamour, and gaming. Some may not know that Las Vegas is the only major city to come into existence in the 20th century, and it wasn't even in Nevada when the state's first boundaries were drawn up in 1864. It was within the Arizona Territory until 1866.

Good thing for Nevada that the boundary was changed. Las Vegas is iconic and so is the "Welcome to Fabulous Las Vegas" sign. Anyone visiting Las Vegas needs to get at least one selfie of themselves standing in front of the popular landmark. To come to Las Vegas and not get a photo at the sign is like visiting Paris and not seeing the Eiffel Tower. Yes, I dare to compare the Vegas sign to the Eiffel Tower.

One Woman's Art

When Betty Jane Willis made the decision not to trademark/copyright her design of the "Welcome to Fabulous Las Vegas" sign, she called it her gift to the city. She probably had no idea how many times the design would be used in Las Vegas advertising and promotion, making it one of the most recognized signs in the world. Betty Jane Willis (1923–2015) was a talented graphic artist in her own right. If you'd like to see more of her early Las Vegas signs, you can find them at the Neon Museum.

The sign was designed in 1959 by graphic artist Betty Jane Willis, who worked for Western Neon, which was under contract to Clark County to create a highway sign that would welcome visitors to Las Vegas. In 2009, 50 years after it was erected, the sign was placed on the National Register of Historic Places.

Located in the median at 5100 Las Vegas Boulevard South, the "Welcome to Fabulous Las Vegas" sign is not all that difficult to find. Park and walk a bit, and be prepared. You may have to stand in line awhile before it's your turn to get up close to the sign; you're not the only tourist in town, after all.

Harrison's Guesthouse

If you would like to experience what it was like to be famous and Black during an era of segregation in the United States, you should take a tour of the Harrison House on Las Vegas's historic West Side at 1001 F Street. Harrison House is listed on the City of Las Vegas's Historic Property Register, the Nevada State Register of Historic Places, and the National Register of Historic Places. Harrison House was owned and operated by Genevieve Harrison, who opened her house in 1942 to traveling celebrities and others who could not get a room in Las Vegas because of their skin color.

Famous entertainers like Sammy Davis Jr., Pearl Bailey, and Nat King Cole, who were entertaining at Las Vegas hotel/casinos but were not permitted to stay the night at the same

Take a Cruise down Sammy Davis Jr. Drive

Today, Las Vegas is one of the most culturally diverse cities in the United States. As hard as it might be to imagine it today, there was a time when Las Vegas was called the Mississippi of the West and Blacks were not permitted to work in the casino industry. Thankfully those days are long gone—and it is good to realize how far we've come. Sammy Davis Jr., who could not stay in Las Vegas hotels at one time, received the honor of having the lights on the Strip dimmed following his death in 1990. Other recipients of such an honor include President John F. Kennedy, President Ronald Reagan, and Frank Sinatra. Another honor that Sammy Davis Jr. was given was to have a Las Vegas street named after him.

establishments, stayed at the Harrison House. Harrison House is the only surviving example of a Las Vegas boardinghouse for Black people during an era of segregation. And that is ironic; on March 1, 1869, Nevada was the first state to ratify the 15th Amendment, which gave voting rights to Black men.

Today, the Harrison House offers tours and serves as a reminder of a shameful time in our state's past and our nation's past as well.

America's Loneliest Road

In Nevada, you don't have to drive very far to get back to nature. We Nevadans might find our open spaces appealing, but others tend to look at the deserts that cover most of the state as monotonous and boring.

Life magazine pointed this fact out in 1986 with an article on the 287-mile stretch of Highway 50 that crosses central Nevada from Fernley to Ely. Highway 50 is part of the Lincoln Highway, built in 1926 to encourage motorists to get out and drive across the county. History buffs take note: Highway 50 parallels the original old Pony Express route. *Life* didn't fully appreciate that and saw only the desolation and called it the "Loneliest Road in America." The name stuck. Almost 30 years have passed, and the road is still lonely; although traffic has increased significantly since that time, it's still not the busy thoroughfare that you might expect.

On certain times of the day, you will cover a lot of asphalt on Highway 50 before you encounter another vehicle. It's just you and the road that stretches on and on and on: lonely to some, heaven to others. It's a fact; Nevada can turn bad press to good (lemons to lemonade) faster than a desert storm can fizzle.

The Nevada Commission on Tourism came up with the "I survived the Loneliest Road in America" promotion. Travelers can buy T-shirts, bumper stickers, and other souvenirs as well as get their US 50 passport stamped every 50 miles or so in the small cities along the highway: Fernley, Fallon, Lovelock, Austin, Eureka, and Ely.

Open Wide, It's a Monster of a Burger

Many of Northern Nevada's historic and unusual sites lie along Highway 50, the Loneliest Road in America. One of those places is the Middlegate Station, about an hour outside of Fallon. The station was established in 1860 as a Pony Express station. This is a unique place to stop and eat with a menu that includes breakfast. Those who are extra hungry can opt for the Middlegate Monster Burger, a triple-decker 1 1/3-pound Angus beef delight that should cure anyone's hunger. Those who can eat it all win a free T-shirt.

If you're tired and sleeping along the Loneliest Road in America seems like a good idea, Middlegate Station offers tent sites, campground sites, and a small motel.

Burlesque Hall of Fame Museum

They were the epitome of ooh-la-la back in the 1940s and '50s. With glamour and glitter, striptease artists like Gypsy Rose Lee, Tempest Storm, Lili St. Cyr, and dozens of others teased, twirled their tassels, and titillated their way across the stage. In doing so, they elevated their talents to a naughty art form known as burlesque. Tame by today's standards, burlesque was downright shocking to our great-grandparents. The Burlesque Hall of Fame Museum is the world's only museum dedicated to the history and art of burlesque.

In today's world of string bikinis that leave little to the imagination and R-rated films that show and tell it all, the striptease hardly seems risqué. If not for the efforts of striptease artist Jennie Lee, the burlesque may have faded into history, stomped out by go-go boots and topless dancers. In 1955, Lee founded the Exotic Dancers League of North America, a dancers' union that helped strippers achieve decent wages.

Along the way, she began amassing a collection of burlesque memorabilia, such as costumes, pasties, and photos. In 1965, she founded the Burlesque Hall of Fame in Helendale, California. Jennie Lee's vision was for the Burlesque Hall of Fame to inspire new dancers, to educate, preserve, and tell the story of burlesque. When she died in 1990, her close friend and former striptease artist, Dixie Evans, continued her work, eventually moving the museum from California to Las Vegas. And that's where you'll find this unique museum, located at 1027 S Main Street, Suite 110, in the art district.

International Car Forest of the Last Church Goldfield

It's art, and it's in the tiny town of Goldfield. Conceived by Nevada artist Chad Sorg and former Goldfield resident Mark Rippie, the idea was to break the Guinness World Record for the world's biggest car forest. The car forest features 40 cars embedded in the dry desert dirt. Most of them feature the artwork of a different artist. Some are whimsical, some perhaps a humorous (or not) political message: for instance, the Ron Paul car, which has been painted over many times by many artists since it was first displayed.

Most old cars end up in the scrapyard but not the cars that are displayed here. These are here for everyone's enjoyment. If you've visited before, you may realize that the cars are the same

and yet this is an ever-changing panoply of art since different artists come to the International Car Forest of the Last Church to paint their unique ideas onto the displayed cars. Now move back from the ant-covered car, a fun place to spend some time. So, if you see a car that you really like, it's best to take a selfie or two, because the next time you happen by, another artist will have changed the car's vibe with his, or her, own ideas. I'm not going to tell you that this is the only car forest in the United States—it's not. But I will tell you that this is the largest. What's more, it's free and open 24/7, and it doesn't get much better than that.

Bugsy Got a Monument

You'd be hard pressed to name any other city in the United States that has a monument commemorating a gangster. But in Las Vegas, a city that has everything, there is a monument to the late mobster. It is dedicated to none other than Benjamin "Bugsy" Siegel. Even though Las Vegas became a city officially in 1905, and Siegel didn't arrive in town until the early 1940s, popular belief holds that Siegel is the father of Las Vegas.

Yes, Bugsy was considered handsome, and he did have some grand-scale ideas of just how a casino should look, and he was the front man who helped to usher the mob into Vegas. And he was instrumental in seeing that the Flamingo Casino opened its doors. Doors that, by the way, are still open; it is in the Rose Garden on the Flamingo grounds that you'll find Bugsy's monument.

Siegel's mugshot from April 12, 1928

The monument stands near the spot where the handsome gangster's penthouse once stood. Nothing left but the memories and the monument, of course. And if you like your ghost stories starring mobsters, there are those who swear on a stack of $50 chips, that the ghostly Bugsy still struts his stuff throughout the area.

Nevada State Prison

I'd be willing to bet that no one goes to prison willingly, with the possible exception of those who work at them. So, what happens to old prisons once they've outlived their usefulness as prisons? Some are torn down and new facilities, parks, or what have you are erected. Old prisons are sometimes repurposed as museums. Such is the case with the old Nevada State Prison. If you're interested in seeing the inside of this old prison, you're in luck. Tours are offered day and night.

The tours last approximately an hour and a half, and while you're getting an inmate's view of the building, the knowledgeable tour guides are ready to fill you in on all the

gruesome details of just what prison life entailed. If ghosts are what you're seeking, be aware that there are special night ghost tours where you just might encounter one of the ghostly inmates who are said to roam this old prison. Susan Bernard and her paranormal group Nevada State Prison Paranormal lead these fun and often spooky tours.

Susan Bernard (bottom left) and some of her Nevada State Prison Paranormal teammates

Seven Come Eleven

Another Nevada first came after Nevada legalized gambling in 1931. So that inmates would have something to occupy their time, the Nevada State Prison became the only prison in the United States to allow the operation of an inmate's casino. Called the Bullpen, the casino was housed in a windowless sandstone building and run entirely by the inmates. Much like any Nevada casino might, the Bullpen offered blackjack, craps, and poker. For their currency, inmates used brass coins in denominations that ranged from five cents to $5. Nothing lasts forever, however; in 1967, a new warden, with new rules and new ideas, took over the prison. One of the first things to go was the Bullpen.

Cui-ui and the Devils Hole Pupfish

Nevada is the only state with bragging rights to an entire family of fish that is found nowhere else on earth. They are the cui-ui of Pyramid Lake and the Devils Hole pupfish of Ash Meadows; they

are the most well known—and the most endangered. Both the cui-ui and Devils Hole pupfish have been affected by climate change and have been on the endangered list since 1967.

The cui-ui, a large sucker fish, can live 40 years, grow to 27 inches in length, and weigh up to seven pounds. The cui-ui was a staple food source of the Native Paiutes for hundreds of years.

Tiny in comparison to the cui-ui, the Devils Hole pupfish attains a length of only three-quarters of an inch. Its habitat is a small 23-feet-by-10-feet cavern in the Ash Meadows National Wildlife Refuge, located about 100 miles west of Las Vegas.

On the brink of extinction in recent years because of lowered water levels, the pupfish has lived in the cavern's 93-degree water for over 20,000 years.

Stratosphere

At 1,149 feet, the Stratosphere Tower in Las Vegas is one for the records. It is the tallest freestanding observation tower in the United States and second-tallest in the Western Hemisphere. But the records don't stop there. The Strat, as locals call it, is the tallest building west of the Mississippi and the tallest structure in Las Vegas.

Thrill seekers don't want to miss a visit to the Stratosphere. First up is SkyJump Las Vegas, a zip line ride that starts at 829 feet above the Las Vegas Strip. Go ahead and jump from the Stratosphere tower; you'll be traveling at speeds of up to 40 miles an hour as you head toward the landing pad. Not scary enough? There are other rides that are sure to give you an adrenaline rush. There are the Big Shot, which shoots riders 160 feet up into the air at speeds of over 45 miles an hour, and X-Scream, the roller coaster that teeters over the top of the Stratosphere. No, thank you. I'll be perfectly content to grab a banana smoothie and gaze out at the Vegas Valley from the observation deck.

With 2,427 rooms and an 80,000-square-foot casino, the Stratosphere is on the north end of the Las Vegas Strip, and is the only Strip hotel casino actually located in Las Vegas. How's that? A little technicality; the Strip is actually in Paradise, an unincorporated town governed by the Clark County Commission. If you're curious, Harry Reid International Airport and the University of Nevada Las Vegas are also located in Paradise.

Fallon Cantaloupe Festival and County Fair

Courtesy alisafarov, iStock

Ever eaten cantaloupe ice cream? Take it from me; it's a tasty way to indulge a love of cantaloupe. And if you're looking for more ways to explore the cantaloupe, this annual event in the fun little town of Fallon is perfect. Held in August, the Fallon Cantaloupe Festival and County Fair is dedicated to agriculture in the region, particularly the different variety of cantaloupes harvested here. Bet you didn't know that there's some rich farmland here in this part of Nevada, did you? Among the offerings are all manner of delicious cantaloupe ideas.

This is also a county fair, so expect a lot of agriculture, arts and crafts, live music, and lots of fun for the kids. If you can sing like Gwen Stefani, only better, you'll get your chance to prove it at one of the karaoke contests.

Gilroy, California, has its Garlic Festival and Fallon has its Cantaloupe Festival. And when you come down to it, wouldn't you rather eat a cantaloupe ice cream cone than a garlic ice cream cone?

See You in the Movies

In addition to being an agricultural community, the small town of Fallon is also where the Naval Air Station Fallon (NAS) is located. Since 1996, NAS has been home to the US Navy-Fighter Weapons School (TOPGUN). If that all sounds familiar, and it should, NAS and the Fallon area played a big role in Tom Cruise's hit movie *Top Gun: Maverick*.

Lion Habitat Ranch in Henderson

Las Vegas's neighboring city, Henderson, surpassed Reno as the second-largest city in Nevada recently. While it's larger than Reno, Henderson is much smaller than Las Vegas. If you happen to be in a certain area of Henderson, you might hear a lion's loud roar. But don't be alarmed; a lion's roar can be heard from up to five miles away and what you're hearing is one of

Courtesy Pieter-Pieter, iStock

the happy lions at the Lion Habitat Ranch. Just as they do in the jungle, lions rule here. But they aren't the only animals in residence.

There are ostriches, parrots, emus—and of course Ozzie, the giraffe who happens to also be an artist. If you're a collector of art, take a look at some of Ozzie's one-of-a-kind paintings that are available for purchase. Yes, I know that there are a zillion things for adults to do in Las Vegas; the Lion Habitat Ranch in Henderson is a fun spot that the kids will also enjoy. And it's only about 15 miles south of the Strip.

Bethel AME Church Reno

The seven-member African Methodist Episcopal congregation of the Bethel AME Church of Reno was organized in 1907. Known as the Biggest Little Church in the West, it is still going strong today and is the longest-operating African American congregation in Nevada.

In 1910, the Reverend William Solley was sent to Reno to oversee the construction of a building for the small congregation. A location at 220 Bell Street was selected. On March 16, 1910, Reverend Solley wrote, we obtained a permit today to build our church on the lot on Bell Street just back of Sheriff Ferrell's home."

There is much history within this church. In 1919, with the congregation steadily increasing, founding members of the church, along with several prominent White people, formed

the first Nevada chapter of the National Association for the Advancement of Colored People (NAACP).

Today, there are more than 100 members of the Bethel AME Church Reno, which is located on Rock Boulevard in Sparks.

The church still owns the historic old church building, which was added to the National Register of Historic Places in 2001. The building is available for rent for events and gatherings.

The Lowdown on the High Roller

Las Vegas's observation wheel dwarfs London's Eye, which is 443 feet tall, and Paris's Roue de Paris (a mere 200 feet tall). Only nine feet taller than the Singapore Flyer, the High Roller, at 550 feet tall, is the world's tallest observation wheel (Ferris wheel). Adorned with 2,000 LED lights that constantly change color, the High Roller at the LINQ is awe inspiring from every vantage point. When the High Roller's 28 glass-enclosed cabins are at capacity, there are 1,120 taking the 30-minute ride. Room for you, your sweetie, the kids, and all your in-laws; tickets won't send you to the poorhouse. Brides looking for someplace unique to share their vows are already eyeing the High Roller.

It's only fitting that the world's tallest Ferris wheel is located in Nevada. After all, George Washington Gale Ferris Jr., the man who invented the Ferris wheel, was from Carson City. Born in

A Ferris Wheel, Shopping and Food

If you're in Northern Nevada and looking for something a bit smaller, head over to Scheels in the Legends at Sparks Marina. It only figures that the world's largest sports store, complete with deli and fudge shop, would offer a ride on the indoor 65-foot Ferris wheel. And after that, you might want to do some serious shopping. Name your favorite department store or trendy boutique and you'll probably find it here at Legends. There are several restaurants to choose from when you want to stop to take a shopping break.

Galesburg, Illinois, on February 14, 1859, George Ferris Jr. was five years old when his family moved to the Carson Valley. As a youth, he spent time near the Cradlebaugh Ranch and its waterwheel. Years later, it would be said that this waterwheel gave young George the idea for his Ferris wheel.

The brand-new Eiffel Tower was a big hit at the International Paris Exposition of 1889. The directors of the World Columbian Exposition decided to outdo Paris, or more specifically, the Eiffel Tower. They offered a challenge to US engineers, a contest to see who could come up with something that would be even more extraordinary. George Ferris Jr. won with his 264-foot Ferris wheel, an instant success when the exposition opened on June 21, 1893.

The Mob Museum, the National Museum of Organized Crime and Law Enforcement

The Mob Museum opened on February 14, 2012. That date coincided with the St. Valentine's Day Massacre that took place in Chicago on Valentine's Day 1929. Seven members of Bugs Moran's gang were lined up against the wall of a garage and shot to death. The killers were never caught, but it was believed that Al Capone may have had a hand in it.

The cold-blooded killings sparked the public's interest in gangsters and their way of life and death. It was a way of life that came to Las Vegas in the 1940s when debonair gangster Benjamin "Bugsy" Siegel convinced his bosses to build and operate the Flamingo Hotel/Casino. Legalized gambling enchanted mobsters, and before long, the mob had its mitts on several Las Vegas casinos. That was a problem that would take several years to clean up and correct.

The public was still fascinated with mobsters, as long as they were, to paraphrase Bugsy Siegel, killing each other. In 1950, the Kefauver hearing into organized crime took place in Las Vegas at the federal courthouse. Today, that courthouse is the building in which the Mob Museum is located. But there are two sides to every story; who were the men and women who kept us safe from the mobsters, who cared about nothing but money and power?

Courtesy of Chon Kit Leong, Dreamstime.com

The good guys' stories needed to be told as well. The Mob Museum presents a balanced view. While you'll learn all about the gangsters like Al Capone, you'll also learn about Eliot Ness and the other people who sought to bring Capone and his cronies to justice.

Plan on spending the day here, and when you get thirsty visit the Underground in the basement where you'll experience an old-time speakeasy.

Grab Your Camera and Have a Seat

Yes, it's macabre. Nonetheless, this chair that came straight out of the Nevada State Prison's now defunct gas chamber is a popular exhibit at the Mob Museum. But then so is an electric chair that you can sit in and power up fake electricity all while taking a selfie or two. Smile as visions of long-ago killers come to mind. It's said that crime doesn't pay and it certainly didn't for those who met their gruesome end in these chairs. You'll hear some of their stories, and those of the lawmen who brought them to justice, at the Mob Museum.

Best in the West Rib Cook Off

Barbecue: the word is magical. This is Sparks's signature event, and one of its oldest as well. The magic happens in Victorian Square downtown every Labor Day weekend. It's September, fall is in the air, and teams of cooks from all around the country come here to prove their prowess with barbecue, and to sell their

ribs. These cooks take their cooking very seriously; they're competing for the coveted Best in the West title, a trophy, and thousands of dollars in cash. But make no mistake, this is a big deal. During the three-day event, a quarter of a million pounds of meat will be lathered in sauce, or dry powdered, and put to the smoker, to eventually be devoured.

Bring the family and come hungry; there will be plenty to eat. Besides all those luscious ribs, there are the fixings. Think slaw, potato salad, corn on the cob, beans, and more. Come ready to dance; there is always live music and entertainment. And if dancing isn't your thing, there is always shopping; lots of unique items are offered for sale during the Best in the West Rib Cook Off event.

2022 winners Jay and Kayce Rathmann—owners of BJ's Nevada Barbecue Company—with their sons Brian (left) and Zach (right)

Brahma Shrine Las Vegas

Let's dispel a myth here for those who think there is nothing but casinos and lights along the Strip. You just might want to rethink that idea. The 14-foot-high Erawan Shrine on the north end of the Roman Plaza outside Caesars Palace is the only Brahma shrine in the Western Hemisphere. And it's been in place here since 1984. Known in Thailand as Phra Prom, the shrine is a replica of the one at the Erawan Hotel in Bangkok. The shrine is said to bring visitors (and thus gamblers) prosperity and good luck. Visitors to the shrine can light incense sticks if they wish to.

Originally created in Bangkok, Thailand, in 1983, the Brahma shrine was donated to Ceasars Palace February 5, 1984, by the Vacharaphol and Hon families. While some Las Vegas visitors may not be aware of the shrine, it has gained in popularity in the last few years. So, expect that you won't be the only person here at the shrine, which is a spectacular site whenever you choose to visit, day or night.

Whose Winchester Was It?

Great Basin National Park located in east central Nevada is a treasure. Among the incredible things to see here are groves of bristlecone pines, the oldest known living non-clonal organisms on earth; the spectacular Lehman Caves; and Wheeler Peak Glacier.

A mystery of sorts began here at the Great Basin National Park on November 6, 2014, when an archaeology team found a Winchester rifle (model 1873) leaning against a juniper tree. The rifle was manufactured in 1882 and is known as "The Gun That Won the West." Obviously, the gun had been here for a very long time. Who did the gun belong to? And why would someone just take off and leave their gun here anyway?

While those are questions likely never to be answered, the rifle was taken to a local hospital to be x-rayed under the

Magnificent Comes to Mind

Centuries before a local prospector by the name of Absalom Lehman discovered the cavern that would be known as the Lehman Caves in the 1880s, ancient Native Americans were using it for burials. The caves have been a place of wonderment ever since. On January 24, 1922, the Lehman Caves was established as a national monument by President Warren Harding. Eleven years later, Franklin Roosevelt put the national monument into the control of the National Park Service. The Lehman Caves is a spectacular site and is enjoyed by hundreds of thousands of visitors from all over the world each year. Guided tours are offered throughout the year.

patient's name of "rifle." After being displayed elsewhere, the Winchester is home once again and on display at the Lehman Caves Visitor Center about five miles north of Baker on the west side of Nevada Highway 487.

The Seven Magic Mountains

This is not at all what you might expect from Las Vegas. But it is well worth a visit. Granted, nature's art is unique and irreplaceable. But what happens when man gives nature a reimagining? This incredible art in the middle of the Nevada desert that was created by renowned Swiss artist Ugo Rondinone in 2011 answers the question. And the result is the colorful, large-scale, site-specific public art installation that is the Seven Magic Mountains. Slated to only be open for a couple years, the Seven Magic Mountains proved so popular that there is talk of making it a permanent display.

Roy and Bonnie Harper stand next to a Seven Magic Mountains figure

Art Is in the Eye of the Beholder

What is art? That is a question not so easily answered because we all have our own ideas of what art is. Some may say art is Vincent van Gogh's *Starry Night*; others may say art is Rodin's *The Kiss*. And then there is land art. During the 1960s and '70s, the emerging art form known as land art was being created at Jean Dry Lake in Southern Nevada by artists like Jean Tinguely and Michael Heizer. Land art, which incorporates the land itself, has gained in popularity as new artists turn their creativity toward the land. The location for Seven Magic Mountains was chosen in a nod toward Land art's early beginnings at Jean Dry Lake.

Located about 10 miles south of Las Vegas near Jean Dry Lake and Interstate 15, Seven Magic Mountains in its bright neon colors won't be easily missed.

And if you're on the lookout for a great place to stop and take a couple of selfies away from the usual Las Vegas stuff, this would be it. What's more, it's free and always open. How often can you say that about something different and unusual, especially in Las Vegas?

The Lost Breyfogle Mine

If not for mining and the subsequent discovery of rich ores, Nevada might never have been. It follows then that the Silver State with all its silver rushes would also have some legends of lost mines and hidden treasure scattered somewhere out in the desert among the sagebrush and sand. In 1863, prospector Charles Breyfogle unwittingly added to Nevada's lost mine lore when he discovered rich ore beyond his wildest dreams.

There are several different versions of the tale of Charles Breyfogle and his lost mine. In March 1863, Breyfogle and two partners struck out for Nevada from Los Angeles.

After making a discovery of gold, the likes of which they'd never seen somewhere in central Nevada, the men packed up their mules and were ready to head back and make their claim. But they were attacked by Indians who killed Breyfogle's two partners but for some reason spared Breyfogle himself.

Someday Some Lucky Person Might Stumble upon It

Yes, there is gold in the Silver State where mining for precious metals and ores still goes on today. Mining helped to make Nevada a state and is embedded deep in the state's history and lore. Of all the stories of miners and their lost mines, the tale of Charles Breyfogle is the most enduring. Is it possible to strike it rich by finding the treasure of a long-dead man? This is Nevada, a state where casinos recently paid out a $14 million slot machine winner, so anything is possible.

He headed to Austin in the eastern part of Nevada, bragging about the gold mine he'd found. Impressed by Breyfogle's gold, several men agreed to accompany him on his quest. But once they got to the area, Charles Breyfogle was unable to find the location of the gold mine he and his partners had stumbled upon. He died out in the desert still trying to locate his lost mine.

Was there ever a mine? Or had Charles Breyfogle exaggerated his tale of gold? No one knows for certain. But people have been attempting to find Breyfogle's lost gold mine ever since he rode into Austin with a saddlebag full of gold.

Courtesy of Salil Bhatt, iStock

Singing Sand Mountain

One of the many things that Nevada has bragging rights to is a mountain that sings. Officially known as Sand Mountain, it is also called Singing Mountain. Okay, there are many other acoustical, booming, or singing dunes in the world. But there aren't many located in North America. California has two and so does Hawaii. And, of course, there is Nevada's Sand Mountain. Lying on the edge of ancient Lake Lahontan along Highway 50, approximately 25 miles east of Fallon, Sand Mountain is three and a half miles long, one mile wide, and 600 feet in height, the largest single dune in the Great Basin. It is a popular site that is managed by the US Department of the Interior and the Bureau of Land Management (BLM). Each year 50,000 to

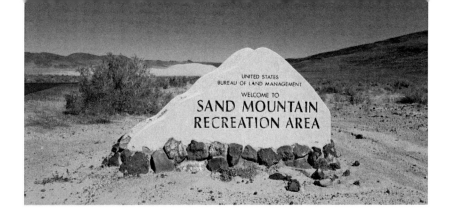

70,000 outdoor enthusiasts visit the 4,795-acre recreational area for camping, hiking, sand boarding, ATVs, motorcycles, sand rails, dune buggies, and side by sides. Sand Mountain is said to be one of the best places in the United States to witness the phenomena of booming or singing dunes. Scientists explain that Sand Mountain sings or booms because of the vibrations and movement of the smooth, rounded grains of sand and the warm, dry climate.

Science has its explanation. But the local Paiute Shoshone peoples have an entirely different idea as to why the mountain sings. According to their beliefs, the singing is actually the sorrowful hissing of Kwasee, an ancient serpent that lived with their people where they were created at the sacred mountain, Fox Peak in the Stillwater Range.

Kwasee and his wife lived happily beneath the Stillwater Mountains; together they journeyed across what is present-day Western Nevada (Pyramid Lake, Lake Tahoe, and Walker Lake) teaching and spreading joy wherever they went. Kwasee's wife died and he was so heartbroken that he buried himself in the sand at the foot of the Stillwater Range; there he remains to this day. According to the elders, Kwasee is still alive beneath Sand Mountain and still continues to bestow his guidance and protection upon them.

Spring Mountain Ranch State Park

While billionaire Howard Hughes was buying up every casino in Las Vegas that he could, he also purchased Spring Mountain Ranch, located about 24 miles from Las Vegas. Owner Vera Krupp had tried to sell the ranch to the US government for use as a park. But Vera wanted a million dollars plus and the government just couldn't do it.

Lucky for Nevadans, Howard Hughes had no problem writing the million-dollar check to Vera, who sold it to him three months before she died in 1967. You can quit all thoughts of Hughes, with a 10-gallon Stetson on his head, riding a thoroughbred across the ranch's acreage. That didn't happen. In fact, Howard

Many visitors to Las Vegas think the Strip is everything that the area has to offer, the be-all and the end-all of Las Vegas. They have no idea about Spring Mountain Ranch State Park and miss out on its breathtaking and rugged beauty. It is hard to imagine such a location in such close proximity to the glamourous Las Vegas. Here is yet another Southern Nevada location in which evidence indicates that Native American ancient peoples lived on this land 10,000 years ago. Later, those traveling to California along the Spanish Trail would stop here and let their animals drink water at one of the many natural springs.

Hughes didn't spend any time here at all. And that's a pity. Spring Mountain Ranch State Park is one of the most scenic spots in Southern Nevada.

Pack a picnic lunch and come for the day. Attend one of the many special events that are presented here. Or just explore and visit the old Krupp house where you'll see and hear about the night Vera was robbed of her 33.6-carat Asscher-cut diamond ring.

Buried Treasure of the Last Stagecoach Robbery

The Old West's last stagecoach robbery took place in 1916 in Jarbidge, a remote little town 10 miles south of the Idaho-Nevada border. Admittedly, Jarbidge is an odd name. If you're wondering where it comes from, it's said to be a Shoshone word, *Tsawhawbitts*, which means "man-eating giant of the canyon." According to Shoshone legend, Tsawhawbitts was an evil giant that lived in the nearby canyon. His days were spent catching unfortunate people, whom he devoured in the evenings. It's also possible that Jarbidge comes from the Nez Perce word for devil, *Jahabich*.

Courtesy of Mark Hufstetler, Wikimedia Commons

Regardless of the origin of its name, Jarbidge enjoyed a brief gold rush when gold was discovered in Jarbidge Canyon in 1909. Gold seekers swarmed the town for what would be the West's last gold rush. As a result, the population rapidly increased. As the gold played out, people packed up and moved on.

By 1916, the gold was long gone and the population, save for a few hearty souls, had dwindled. On December 5, 1916, a heavy snowstorm hit the canyon. But it wasn't enough to stop the mail wagon from Rogerson, Idaho, from coming through. Just outside of town, the coach was robbed and its driver, Frank Searcy, shot to death. The killer made off with a bag of double-eagle gold coins valued at $4,000. It would be hours before the wagon and Searcy's body were discovered.

The killer was eventually apprehended and sent to prison. But what did he do with that bag of gold coins? He didn't admit to the crime and claimed he didn't know anything about where it might be found. Although people have been searching for that bag and its gold coins ever since, it's never been found. That's what they say anyway.

There's Luck, and Then There's Luck

Ben Kuhl was arrested and convicted for the robbery of the Jarbidge stagecoach and the murder of its driver. His 1917 trial was the first US case in which palm prints were used as evidence in a court of law. This set a precedent that palm prints are as valid in identification as fingerprints are. Sentenced to death, Kuhl chose to die by firing squad. With luck on his side, his sentence was commuted to life in prison by the Nevada Board of Pardons. He spent 28 years in prison before his release in 1945.

Chapter Six

The Dark and Naughty Side of Nevada

Every state has its naughty side. Nevada's may be a little bit naughtier than most being the only state in the US with legalized prostitution. Prostitute Julia Bulette was murdered in her bed, giving the red light lady legendary status. Julia is still revered in Virginia City more than a century after her death. Nevada has executed only one woman in its history. Elizabeth Pitts holds the dubious distinction of being the one and only.

. . . .

The First and Only Woman Nevada Executed

With the unlikely name of Elizabeth Potts, you might see her as anything but a murderer. But murderer she was, and she holds the honor (if indeed it is such) of being the only woman executed by the state of Nevada.

Elizabeth Potts was not a particularly attractive woman, and some could argue if she'd been otherwise, she might never have walked those 13 steps to the gallows. But she wasn't and she did. Her victim was Miles Faucett. With the help of her husband, Josiah, Faucett's body was dismembered, burned, and buried in the basement of the Potts's rental home in the tiny eastern Nevada town of Carlin.

Not a Ghost of a Chance

Mr. Faucett might be resting in peace after Elizabeth Potts was hanged for his murder. But that might not be the case with Mrs. Potts herself. Stories of her ghostly presence haunting the Elko County Courthouse, and the area surrounding the court, have been told almost from the day of her death in 1889.

But murder will come out. And the body came to light, some say, because Faucett's ghost would not rest until Elizabeth Potts was brought to justice. On June 30, 1889, the ghostly Faucett got his wish—Elizabeth Potts and her husband, Josiah, after having been found guilty, were hanged one after the other, behind the old Elko County Courthouse.

Dubious Distinctions

We've already seen the dubious distinction that Elizabeth Potts holds as the first and only woman executed by the state of Nevada, but there are others. Nevada was the first state to use the gas chamber as a means of executing those who were handed down death sentences. Gee Jon has the questionable honor of being the first person to be so dispatched. In 1921, the Nevada State Legislature approved lethal gas for use in executions. Three years later, on February 8, 1924, Jon walked into the gas chamber at the Nevada State Prison in Carson City. Within minutes he was a dead man. The gas chamber proved successful, and the executions continued. The youngest person ever executed by the state of Nevada was 17-year-old Floyd Loveless in 1944. Loveless was convicted of the shooting death of Carlin Constable A. H. Berning.

Floyd Loveless. Courtesy of Nevada State Library and Archives

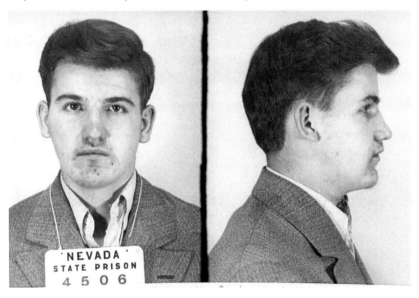

The oldest person executed by the state of Nevada was 61-year-old John Kramer, who went to the gas chamber on August 28, 1942, for the murder of his girlfriend Frances Collins.

Singer-actor Frank Sinatra is the only celebrity to have had his Nevada gaming license snatched by the state. This is because Sinatra committed a big no-no and broke Nevada's gaming rules when he permitted mobster Sam Giancana to stay at his Cal Neva Lodge in Lake Tahoe in 1962. But don't feel too bad for Sinatra. President Reagan gave him a glowing reference in the 1980s and his gaming license was reinstated.

When he was killed in a Las Vegas drive-by shooting in 1997, rapper Tupac Shakur became the only celebrity to have been murdered in the state of Nevada. His murder remains unsolved.

Politics and Prostitution

Nevada is the only state that permits legalized prostitution. Like gaming, tourism, and mining, legalized prostitution is a fact of life here in Nevada. Whether one agrees or disagrees, these businesses pay as much as $100,000 for a yearly license and hefty taxes. Everyone is happy. For all that, the state's two largest counties, Clark (Las Vegas) and Washoe (Reno), long ago decided not to allow legalized prostitution. Other counties in which prostitution is banned are Douglas and Lincoln.

Oddly, or maybe not, those who work in Nevada's sex-for-pay industry sometimes jump into politics. Storey County Commissioner Lance Gilman is the most recent to enter politics. Businessman Gilman, owner of the Mustang Ranch Brothel, is the first owner of such a business to be elected to public office. The popular Republican won by 62 percent of the vote.

Pretty Jessi Winchester, a redhead from Iowa, really stirred things up when she competed in the Mrs. Nevada contest, representing Virginia City in 1995. Although she tried to keep her job at one of the local brothels hush-hush, word soon got out. And it garnered worldwide attention for her. Never mind that she held a legal job at a legal establishment in Storey County. Through it all, Winchester held her head high. After losing the Mrs. Nevada contest, she ran for the US House of Representatives in 1996. Placing second in the primaries only spurred her on. In 1998, she ran for Lieutenant Governor and lost.

"I think it takes a madam of an honest bordello to show them how to run an honest system," Cottontail Ranch (brothel) owner Beverly Harrell said before running for the Nevada State

Madame Beverly Harrell's
World Famous Legal Bordello

The Cottontail Ranch

• Bar Open 24 Hours • 2 Mile Airstrip
Established Since 1967

1 (775) 572-3111
Pay Phone Lida #2

Nevada

Assembly in 1974. The Cottontail Ranch sat on land that was actually owned by the federal government. The Bureau of Land Management (BLM) leased the land to Harrell for $100 a year. That is, until it became public knowledge. Then all bets were off. The BLM wasted no time in evicting Harrell and her Cottontail Ranch. But not to worry; she continued her operation mere yards away.

Dead Man Running

Flamboyant and opinionated, Dennis Hof owned a string of brothels from one end of Nevada to the other. The star of the HBO reality TV series *Cathouse*, Hof thrived on publicity. And he knew how to get it. From his Hookers for Hillary campaign during the 2016 presidential race to his Alien Cathouse on Highway 95, Hof was always good for a story on a slow news day.

But hookers or not, Hillary lost. Donald Trump was elected president and politics changed. Suddenly a president was saying and doing things that no other president had ever done before. Dennis Hof took note. He had a large ego and a matching bank account. And he dove into politics, letting it be known that he was the Trump of Pahrump. And as a Republican, he was running for state assembly in Nevada's District 36. Some of those who knew him best said it was all a publicity stunt and that he cared less about politics than he did about morality.

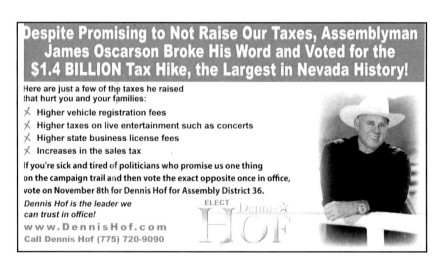

A Man and His Secrets

Dennis Hof loved the limelight. Wherever the cameras were, that's where he wanted to be. And that brings up the story of Hof and his Louis Vuitton bag. One afternoon, he went into a television interview, leaving the Vuitton on a small sofa in the waiting room where other guests awaited their turn before the camera. After his interview concluded, Hof strolled out the door to his oh-so-expensive sports car parked just outside the large window. He slid into the driver's seat and quickly jumped back out. Running into the waiting room, he exclaimed, "My Louis Vuitton—my Louis Vuitton!"

Another guest pointed to the costly bag still sitting where Hof had placed it. Hof grabbed the bag and raced out the door, leaving all to wonder what was in the bag.

We'll never know for sure. Dennis Hof died in his sleep on October 16, 2018. That was a mere three weeks before the November 6 election day. Oh, what to do, what to do? It was too late to change the ballots; they'd already been printed. So, there he was, Dennis Hof, dead man running for public office. He probably would have liked the weirdness of it all. Oddly enough, Hof, dead as he was, won the election.

Julia Bulette

There is also the fabled side of prostitution. You know, the woman of low morals with the heart of gold . . . Virginia City courtesan Julia Bulette is without a doubt Nevada's most famous such prostitute. She might have been forgotten with time, if not for the fact that on a cold winter night in January 1867 the unfortunate Julia was bludgeoned to death while she slept.

A town favorite (of the male population anyway), Virginia City vowed there would be justice. After a funeral, the likes of which had never been seen in Virginia City, the search

Only in Virginia City

Alexia Sober, owner of the Canvas Café in Virginia City, had a problem. There was a dead tree on her property right in front of the café. She decided something unique needed to be done about the tree. And after giving it some thought, she commissioned a local artist to turn the dead tree trunk into a statue of Julia Bulette. The resulting statue faces eastward toward her final resting place and the area where her crib once stood. In putting the dead tree into an artist's hands, Alexia created a tourist attraction and lent a bit more uniqueness to Virginia City. How many cities do you know that have a statue on the main street of a local historical personage who happened to be a lady of the evening?

for Julia's killer intensified. A Frenchman by the name of John Millian was arrested for the crime (he was trying to sell her jewels and her dress patterns). Although he denied the deed, and his case went all the way to the Nevada Supreme Court, John

Fragment of rope used to hang John Millian, the murderer of Julia Bulette, Virginia City, April 24, 1868

Millian was tried and convicted of killing Julia. He hanged for the crime in April 1868. And wouldn't you know it? Mark Twain was in Virginia City at the time of the execution and wrote a report on Millian's hanging. If you'd like a glimpse of an odd historic artifact, you should know that a piece of the rope used in Millian's execution is on display at the Nevada State Capitol Building in Carson City.

Pyramid Lake.
Courtesy of Library of Congress

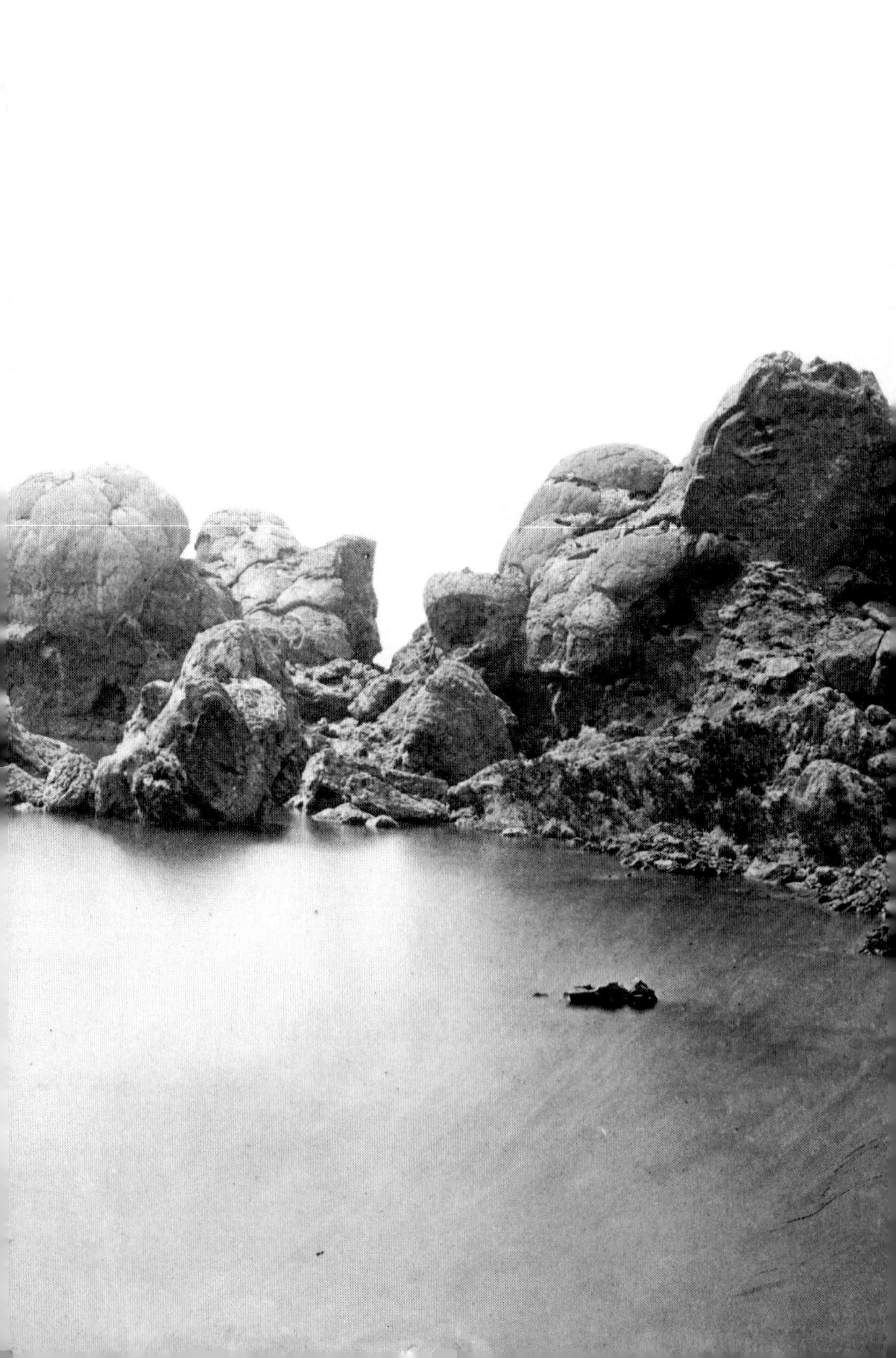

Chapter Seven

Nevada Legends and Lore

Nevada is enriched by many cultures. Because of this, it is a state rich in legends and lore. Many of its legends spring from the Native American people that lived here centuries before the Europeans arrived. The mysterious Ong of Lake Tahoe and the Water Babies of Pyramid Lake are two such legends. Miners from around the world brought their legends and superstitions to Nevada.

The Ong

According to Native American legend, the Ong was a giant bird that regularly rose out of the beautiful mountain lake we know today as Lake Tahoe. The evil Ong devoured any unlucky humans it happened upon. This monster bird had the face of a human that was covered with hard scales. Its body was that of an eagle with webfeet and wings that was taller than the tallest pines. The Ong's nest was in the deepest part of the lake, directly in the center.

The Ong favored human flesh, but being a coward, it attacked only children, women, or hunters who happened to be alone. Like all monsters, the Ong had a vulnerable spot. It had no claws or beak. While the Ong had no fear of arrows

that couldn't pierce his feathers or of the strongest spears that bounced off the scales of his face and legs, he lived in constant fear that someone might discover his weakness of having no claws and beak.

Tahoe was the young man who wanted to marry the chief's beautiful daughter. But so did every other young man in the village. If not for his bravery in fighting and slaying the Ong, Tahoe would not have gained the chief's admiration and been permitted to marry the chief's daughter.

But I've jumped ahead of events—Tahoe watched as the Ong rose out of the lake and neared the village's celebration. This was his one chance. And he took it. Tahoe allowed himself to be grabbed by the Ong so that he could take advantage of the bird's lack of claws and beak.

In slaying the Ong, Tahoe proved his worth and was married to the chief's daughter. He was also honored with the lake being named after him.

Pyramid Lake

Native Americans had been living by the lake known as Cui-ui Pah in the Northern Nevada desert for thousands of years when explorer John C. Fremont and his party came upon the lake during Fremont's 1844 exploration of the Great Basin. As the first European descendants to discover the lake, the men were impressed with the vast salt lake and its tufa formations.

John Fremont dubbed the lake Pyramid Lake and wrote of it:

> It rose, according to our estimate about 600 feet above the water, and from the point we viewed it, presented a pretty exact outline of the great pyramid of Cheops. Like other rocks along the shore, it seemed to be encrusted with calcareous cement. This striking feature suggested a name for the lake and I called it Pyramid Lake.

Located 42 miles north of Reno, Pyramid Lake is 188.03 square miles, which is the largest portion of what remains of the prehistoric Inland Sea Lake Lahontan that covered most of Nevada thousands of years ago.

There are many Native American legends associated with the lake that John C. Fremont and his party never heard. One of the most often told is that of creatures known as the Water Babies. Fair warning, while this sounds like a pleasant story, it is not. The Water Babies are known to pull unsuspecting people to their deaths in the murky waters' depths. The story holds that it's not wise to talk or sing loudly at dusk while walking the shoreline at Pyramid Lake.

Yet another legend involves the cui-ui fish that are endemic to Pyramid Lake. According to that legend, the cui-ui are also

For the Birds

Weather permitting, sunbathing, swimming, fishing, and boating are all enjoyable activities at Pyramid Lake. But take note: boats aren't permitted within 1,000 feet of Anaho Island refuge, and it is closed to the public. Established by President Woodrow Wilson in 1913, the Anaho Island National Wildlife Refuge is located on Anaho Island in Pyramid Lake and is part of the Pyramid Lake Paiute Reservation. It contains one of the two largest colonies of American white pelicans in the western United States.

found in a large body of water in Africa. Why is that? Well, according to the story, it is because there is a secret underground waterway linking Pyramid Lake to the body of water in Africa.

Jacques Cousteau Couldn't Say

Every year an estimated 15 million visitors come to Lake Tahoe. The lake is the largest alpine lake on the North American continent; it contains enough water to cover the entire state of California with 14 inches of water. Lake Tahoe is also noted for the clarity of its waters. One of the world's most beautiful lakes, it's no wonder that since the first Native Americans made their homes here, legends and stories have surrounded the lake.

One of those stories involves oceanographer Jacques Cousteau. There are as many different versions of this story as there are photos of Lake Tahoe. Most anyone at Lake Tahoe will tell you about their favorite version. The story stems from the

What Is in a Name?

What's in a name? Shakespeare said that a rose by any other name would smell as sweet—so it is with lakes. Lake Tahoe has been known by other names. In 1844, it was called Lake Bonpland. In 1854, the lake was officially named Lake Bigler after then California Governor John Bigler. Not everyone was pleased with this name. But Mark Twain was. In 1863, he wrote an article proclaiming the name Bigler as the correct name and not Tahoe, which he said meant grasshopper soup. The Bigler versus Tahoe name argument continued until 1945 when the California Legislature reversed itself and officially named the lake Tahoe.

Courtesy of Jropelato2 via Dreamstime.com

tale of the exploration of the lake that Cousteau was said to have made in a submersible craft. Rumors flew. According to some it was a matter of national security, others had the CIA at Cousteau's doorstep, demanding the evidence he'd discovered at the bottom of the lake. Imaginations ran wild. The most outlandish claimed that Cousteau saw UFOs and prehistoric creatures.

The truth is Monsieur Cousteau didn't see anything because he never visited Lake Tahoe. It was Cousteau's son Philippe who did the exploring of Lake Tahoe. He didn't see anything out of the ordinary, save for the perfectly preserved bodies of drowning victims and ancient trees—that's how the story goes. I'll leave it up to the reader to form his, or her, own opinions as to just how much of this Tahoe tale is legend or fact.

Butch Cassidy Did What in Winnemucca?

Butch Cassidy and the Sundance Kid achieved legendary status not only for their train-robbing exploits but also for the classic 1969 film *Butch Cassidy and the Sundance Kid* that told the story of the two outlaws.

It's a great film, regardless of how far the truth was stretched in its making. The same holds true for the tale that Winnemucca loves to share about that time the outlaws, or at least Butch and the gang, rode into town.

It's a good story. And tourists love hearing about how Butch, Sundance, and the Wild Bunch rode into Winnemucca with bank robbing on their minds. But it wasn't Butch Cassidy who robbed the First National bank of $32,000 at high noon on September 19, 1900. According to Nevada legend and lore, Cassidy planned the whole thing and was involved in the heist up to his sidearm.

Butch Cassidy (bottom right), "the Sundance Kid" Harry Alonzo Longabaugh (bottom left), and the gang

From Millionaire to Politician

The bank cashier who was robbed at gunpoint by the Wild Bunch gang that day in 1900 was George S. Nixon. Nixon left Winnemucca shortly after the robbery and went on to become an important politician, US Senator from Nevada, in 1905; he served until his death from meningitis in 1912. Nixon mentored and later partnered with George Wingfield and they formed the Goldfield Consolidated Mines, which had a value of $25 million. While Wingfield built the Goldfield Hotel, Nixon built the Nixon Bank in Goldfield.

But it simply isn't so, according to former Nevada archivist and mythbuster Guy Rocha. There is evidence that Cassidy was hundreds of miles away in Tipton, Wyoming, a few days before the Winnemucca bank holdup. Doing what? Why, robbing a train, of course. Lest you think it's all a tall tale, the Sundance Kid and the rest of the Wild Bunch gang probably did rob the bank in Winnemucca. Whoever it was, they got away clean with the loot; there were never any arrests made in the case.

Tom Peasley, the Man Who Killed His Killer

In 1860, Tom Peasley came to Virginia City from San Francisco. Within the year, the well-liked Peasley had established himself in the community, as being valuable to the town that lacked ability to fight fires.

Fire was one of the most serious threats facing towns like Virginia City. Peasley, having been a part of San Francisco's fire departments, helped organize the Virginia Fire Company No. 1 and Nevada Hook and Ladder Company No. 1. Peasley also helped organize Nevada's first fire department, the Virginia Fire Department.

Tom Peasley

On the night of September 20, 1863, Tom Peasley encountered Jack Jenkins (aka Sugarfoot) in Pat Lynch's Niagara Saloon and Dance Hall. Peasley playfully shoved Jenkins, who didn't take kindly to the playful gesture. When Peasley left the saloon, Jenkins followed him out. Peasley, believing the other man was armed, turned and shot him where he stood. Jenkins dropped dead—he was not armed.

Self-defense—charged with murder, Tom was found not guilty and walked out of the court a free man January 7, 1865.

Second Hand Firearm

Did Tom Peasley's gun carry a curse? Some believed it did. According to a story that appeared in the Gold Hill News on February 19, 1864, Peasley owned the gun that had killed two notorious bad men: Jack Williams and Jack Reeder. A gunslinger known as Sugarfoot Jack was hunting for Tom Peasley while armed with this same gun. Unfortunately for Sugarfoot, Peasley got the drop on him and put an end to his nefarious plan. Strange as it may seem, the gun that was meant to be used in his murder was given to Peasley by a friend in law enforcement.

The following year on February 2, 1866, Peasley was in Carson City drinking with friends at the Ormsby House. Unfortunately, Martin Barnhart was among those drinking at the Ormsby House that night. He did not like Tom Peasley. The previous year Peasley had shot him in the leg during a disagreement.

Calling Peasley a coward, Barnhart drew his gun and shot Peasley in the chest twice. Mortally wounded, Peasley dropped to the floor. But even as he lay dying, Peasley would have his revenge; he pulled his gun and shot Barnhart in the back three times as the other man fled. In his dying breath, Peasley asked friends to remove his boots. No one in the Old West wanted to die with their boots on.

Peasley's bullets had found their mark and he had killed his killer; Barnhart was found dead a short while later.

In 1997, Tom Peasley was named a Distinguished Service Recipient by the Professional Fire Fighters of Nevada.

Spring Mountain Ranch State Park

Sources

Nevada's Amazing People

The Ancestral Puebloans: Ancestral Puebloan - Science of the American Southwest (US National Park Service) (nps.gov)

Sarah Winnemucca: https://www.britannica.com/biography/Sarah-Winnemucca

Charlie Chaplin's Leading Lady: Edna Purviance https://www.ednapurviance.org/index.html

Nevada Politicians: https://www.history.com/topics/us-presidents/ronald-reagan; https://www.britannica.com/biography/Pat-Nixon

Hizzoner, the Mayor: https://renodivorcehistory.org/themes/law-of-the-land/legal-personalities/; https://www.vegaslegalmagazine.com/oscar-goodman-the-first-king-of-las-vegas/

Mark Twain: https://travelnevada.com/historical-interests/forget-what-you-heard-nevada-is-the-true-birthplace-of-mark-twain/

Rafael Rivera: The Man Who Named Las Vegas: https://www.lasvegasnevada.gov/News/Blog/Detail/who-is-rafael-rivera

The Mysterious Queho: https://www.mysterywire.com/true-crime/the-twisted-tale-of-queho-the-last-renegade-indian/

Anne Henrietta Martin: https://nevadawomen.org/research-center/biographies-alphabetical/anne-henrietta-martin/

Eilley Bowers: https://nevadawomen.org/research-center/biographies-alphabetical/alison-eilley-oram-bowers/

Howard Hughes: https://www.biography.com/business-leaders/howard-hughes

Paranormal Nevada

Virginia City: https://visitvirginiacitynv.com/

The Washoe Club: https://www.thewashoeclubmuseum.com/

Goldfield Hotel: https://travelnevada.com/hotels/historic-goldfield-hotel/

Miss Dana's Tea Shoppe and the Eureka Tunnels: https://www.visiteurekanevada.net/historical-ghost-tours

Zak Bagans's Haunted Museum: https://thehauntedmuseum.com/

Nevada Out of This World

Nellis Air Force Base: https://www.wearethemighty.com/mighty-culture/the-complete-base-guide-to-nellis-air-force-base/

Of Atomic Bombs: https://www.britannica.com/place/Area-51

The Conqueror **and the Red Sand:** A Stunning Number Of The Conqueror's Cast And Crew Developed Cancer (grunge.com); https://www.thevintagenews.com/2018/02/19/the-conqueror-film/?edg-c=1

Ely's UFO Crash Site: https://elyufocrash.com/

Flying Saucers over the Biggest Little City . . . and Beyond: https://www.nevadaappeal.com/news/2013/dec/19/are-ufos-flying-over-northern-nevada/

Extraterrestrial Highway: https://spacetourismguide.com/extraterrestrial-highway/

Little A'Le'Inn in Rachel: https://www.wired.com/story/rachel-nevada-area-51/

The Mysterious McDermitt Lights: http://www.astronomycafe.net/weird/lights/mcdermott2.html

Alien Research Center: https://www.visittheusa.com/experience/driving-nevadas-extraterrestrial-highway-otherworldly-experience

Atomic Museum Vegas: https://www.atomicmuseum.vegas/

That's Quirky, Nevada

The Skulls of Patrick and Susan Clayton: https://lasvegassun.com/news/1999/oct/19/grave-robber-gets-probation-for-theft-of-skull/

Black Rock City: https://burningman.org/event/

Wild Horses and Burros: https://travelnevada.com; https://pvtimes.com/news/beattys-burros-both-an-old-west-symbol-and-a-problem/

Somewhere in Time, Maude: https://www.tandfonline.com/doi/abs/10.1080/10400419.2005.9651488

The Baskets of Dat So La Lee: https://americanindian.si.edu/exhibitions/infinityofnations/california-greatbasin/118261.html

Double Negative **and** *City*: https://travelnevada.com/arts-culture/double-negative/

Joshua Trees: https://powo.science.kew.org/taxon/urn:lsid:ipni.org:names:270297-2; https://blog.tentree.com/10-facts-about-the-incredible-joshua-tree/

Rustlin' Shoes: https://lrheaultrsj.wordpress.com/2017/10/23/bovine-ingenuity/

Liberace Lived on Shirley Avenue: https://theliberacemansion.com/the-story-2/

Ghost, the Dog: https://www.usatoday.com/story/news/nation/2023/02/14/ghost-coyote-dog-reunited-family-hades/11256504002/ https://www.fox5vegas.com/2023/02/03/ghosts-story-elusive-white-dog-spotted-living-with-coyote-pack-henderson/

Ethel M. Chocolate Factory and Botanical Cactus Garden: https://www.tripadvisor.com/Attraction_Review-g45953-d145286-Reviews-Ethel_M_Chocolates_Factory_and_Cactus_Garden-Henderson_Nevada.html

Bing Crosby's Denim Tuxedo: https://www.sfgate.com/entertainment/article/Unraveling-a-mystery-Where-is-Bing-Crosby-s-5694622.php

Goldwell Open Air Museum at Rhyolite: https://www.goldwellmuseum.org/

Clown Motel: https://www.theclownmotelusa.com/

Ward Charcoal Ovens State Historic Park: https://parks.nv.gov/parks/ward-charcoal-ovens

The Man Who Was Hanged Three Times: https://truewestmagazine.com/article/austin-nevada/

Rocky Mountain Oyster Fry: https://visitvirginiacitynv.com/events/rocky-mountain-oyster-fry/

Berlin-Ichthyosaur State Park: https://travelnevada.com/parks-recreational-areas/berlin-ichthyosaur-state-park/

Three Unique Courthouses: https://travelnevada.com/historical-interests/historic-esmeralda-county-courthouse/; https://www.hmdb.org/m.asp?m=22007; https://noehill.com/nv_pershing/nat1986001077.asp.

Fremont Street Experience: https://vegasexperience.com/

Bliss Dance: https://www.marcocochranesculpture.net/bliss-dance; https://www.marcocochranesculpture.net/bliss-project

Thunderbird Lodge: https://thunderbirdtahoe.org/

Hoover Dam: https://www.britannica.com/topic/Hoover-Dam

Ely's Murals: https://travelnevada.com/historical-interests/renaissance-village-and-ely-mural-walking-tour/; https://elynevada.net/project/public-art/

The Architecture of Paul Revere Williams: https://virtualglobetrotting.com/map/la-concha-motel-lobby-by-paul-r-williams/view/google/; https://www.paulrwilliamsproject.org/index.html.1.72.html

Early Days on the Silver Screen: https://www.imdb.com/name/nm0068471/bio; https://www.britannica.com/biography/Clara-Bow; https://www.britannica.com/topic/The-Misfits

Blue Jeans: https://www.smithsonianmag.com/smithsonian-institution/the-origin-of-blue-jeans-89612175/

In Cold Blood's **Connection to Nevada:** https://themobmuseum.org/blog/sixty-years-later-in-cold-blood-murders-still-resonate/

Genoa's Candy Dance: https://www.genoanevada.org/visitors/candy_dance/index.php

Nevada Things to See and Do

"Welcome to Fabulous Las Vegas" Sign: https://www.tripsavvy.com/welcome-to-fabulous-las-vegas-sign-4778945

Harrison's Guesthouse: https://www.harrisonhouselv.org/about; https://www.nps.gov/places/harrison-s-guest-house.htm

America's Loneliest Road: https://loneliestroad.us/

Burlesque Hall of Fame Museum: https://www.burlesquehall.com/

International Car Forest of the Last Church Goldfield: https://internationalcarforestofthelastchurch.com/

Nevada State Prison: https://mynews4.com/news/knowing-nevada/knowing-nevada-the-paranormal-at-the-nevada-state-prison

Cui-ui and the Devils Hole Pupfish: https://www.nps.gov/deva/learn/nature/devils-hole.htm

Stratosphere: https://www.lasvegas-entertainment-guide.com/stratosphere-rides.html

Fallon Cantaloupe Festival and County Fair: https://www.falloncantaloupefestival.com/

Lion Habitat Ranch in Henderson: https://lionhabitatranch.org/

Bethel AME Church Reno: https://www.blackpast.org/african-american-history/bethel-ame-church-reno-nevada-1907/

The Lowdown on the High Roller: https://www.caesars.com/linq/things-to-do/attractions/high-roller

The Mob Museum, the National Museum of Organized Crime and Law Enforcement: https://themobmuseum.org/

Best in the West Rib Cook Off: https://www.visitrenotahoe.com/featured-events/guide-to-nugget-rib-cook-off-sparks-nevada/

Brahma Shrine Las Vegas: http://www.markslasvegas.com/brahma-shrine/

Whose Winchester Was It?: https://elkodaily.com/forgotten-winchester-returns-to-nevada/article_ab6f64d7-9022-57ba-8823-db896d1f05db.html

The Seven Magic Mountains: https://sevenmagicmountains.com/

The Lost Breyfogle Mine: https://www.desertusa.com/desert-people/charles-breyfogle.html; https://www.nevadaappeal.com/news/2017/oct/13/legends-of-johnnie-and-the-lost-breyfogle-mine/

Singing Sand Mountain: https://www.onlyinyourstate.com/nevada/singing-sands-of-nv/

Spring Mountain Ranch State Park: https://parks.nv.gov/parks/spring-mountain-ranch

Buried Treasure of the Last Stagecoach Robbery: https://www.scribd.com/doc/48988148/America-s-Last-State-Robbery-in-1916-in-Jarbidge-Nevada#; https://www.grunge.com/425418/this-was-the-last-stagecoach-robbery-in-the-wild-west/

The Dark and Naughty Side of Nevada

The First and Only Woman Nevada Executed: https://nevadamagazine.com/issue/may-june-2017/6713/

Dead Man Running: https://www.nbcnews.com/news/us-news/dennis-hof-nevada-brothel-owner-assembly-candidate-died-heart-attack-n988721

Julia Bulette: https://www.historynet.com/miners-virginia-city-julia-bulette-beloved-queen-comstock/

Nevada Legends and Lore

The Ong: https://nevadamagazine.com/issue/november-december-2019/11677/

Pyramid Lake: https://pyramidlake.us/

Jacques Cousteau Couldn't Say: https://www.kqed.org/quest/22882/rumors-and-truth-in-lake-tahoe

Butch Cassidy Did What in Winnemucca?: https://nevadagram.com/butch-cassidy-and-the-great-winnemucca-bank-robbery/

Tom Peasley, the Man Who Killed His Killer: https://www.facebook.com/groups/Oldwestvirginiacity/posts/10158580950341845/

Index